W9-DGF-874

AMERICAN INDIAN DANCES

Steps, Rhythms, Costumes
and Interpretation

John L. Squires
UNIVERSITY OF UTAH

and

Robert E. McLean
SALT LAKE CITY
PUBLIC SCHOOL SYSTEM

Illustrations by Robert E. McLean

THE RONALD PRESS COMPANY • NEW YORK

Library of Congress Catalog Card Number: 63-19746

Preface

"American Indian Dances—Steps, Rhythms, Costumes, and Interpretation" was written with several important objectives in mind, the first of which was to provide a simple and practical book for the teaching of authentic Indian dances. This book supplies source material from which Indian dances can be easily learned and develops dance programs with variation, authenticity, proper theme, costumes, and interpretation; it will help the average dancer and layman to perform, teach, and understand the true purpose and meaning of Indian dancing.

This book is also intended to preserve Indian dances which over the years are being forgotten and to help even Indians themselves to learn, remember, and perpetuate their dances. Still another objective of this book is to help readers make their own inexpensive, yet authentic Indian dance apparel or outfits.

After many months of study, the authors selected twenty-three dances they felt were simple and introductory yet typical of many tribes and representative of many different categories or types of Indian dances. The authors have presented each dance as closely to the true Indian style as possible according to their knowledge and understanding.

The authors wish to thank many Indian tribes, individual Indians, and the Intertribal Pow Wow Group, who so kindly gave information concerning the themes, steps, and patterns of their dances. Also, they wish to thank Mr. LeRoy Condie for his part in kindling their interest in Indian dancing, and Dr. Elizabeth Hayes, head of the dance section of the Department of Health, Physical Education and Recreation at the University of Utah, and her associates, who gave valuable suggestions and encouragement in the development of this book.

ROBERT McLEAN
JOHN L. SQUIRES

Salt Lake City, Utah
   April, 1963

iii

Contents

CHAPTER   PAGE

1   INTRODUCTION 3

2   INDIAN OUTFITS AND HOW TO MAKE THEM 8
     Bolero 10
     Bands—Arm, Head, Leg 11
     Bells—Ankle 12
     Bells—Leg 13
     Bonnet—War or Feathered 14
     Breechclout 16
     Bustle—Feathered 17
     Cuffs 19
     Dress—Squaw 20
     Fetlocks 21
     Leggings 22
     Moccasins 23
     Rattles 25
     Roach—Feathered 26
     Roach—Hair or Fiber 27
     Shirt—War 29
     Yoke 31
     Miscellaneous 32
     Basic Indian Designs:
         Apache 34
         Northwest 34
         Eastern and Southeastern Woodland . . . 35
         Navajo 35
         Plains 36
         Pueblo 37
         Yuma 38

3   BASIC INDIAN DANCE STEPS 39
     Standard Starting Position 39
     One-Foot Stomp 41
     Heel—Toe Step 42
     Toe—Heel Step 43
     Heel Shuffle 44

CHAPTER   PAGE

Foot-and-Heel Shuffle 45
Four-Beat Stomp 46
War Dance Step 47
War Dance Step—Variation 48
Canoe Step 49
Cross-Over Sti-yu 50
Pawing Step 51

4 NATURE DANCES 52
Buffalo—Plains 52
Dying Eagle—Plains 56
Flower—Pueblo: Jemez 60
Horsetail—Taos 63
Hunting—Pawnee 67
Mountain Sheep—Piute 71
Snake—Nambee 75

5 RELIGIOUS DANCES 78
Chief—Sioux 78
Devil, or Gan—Apache 81
Rain—Zuni 84

6 SOCIAL AND COMIC DANCES 88
Belt—Pueblo: Tewa 88
Lost Tomahawk—Plains 92
Old Man—Eastern Woodland 96
Rabbit or Round—Southwest and Plains 99
Squaw—Navajo 102

7 WAR AND SKILL DANCES 107
Bow and Arrow—Southwest 107
Feather—Plains 110
Hoop—Most Tribes 113
Rattle—Plains 117
Scalp—Sioux 120
Shake—Shoshone 123
Spear and Shield—Plains 125
War—Kiowa 129

KEY TO SYMBOLS

In the Basic Step Diagrams

◁◯ Using the full weight of the foot.

◑ Using only the ball of the foot.

◁ Using only the heel of the foot.

◁Ⓛ
◁Ⓡ *L* and *R* designate which foot.

——→ Indicates the direction of movement.

↑ ↓ Indicates the lifting and replacing of the foot.

In Drum-Beat Notations

4/4 | ♪ ♩ ♪ ♩ | 160 This sample notation is the one for the One-Foot Stomp, one of the basic dance steps given a detailed description in Chapter 3. (For full explanation of the various notations, see the list of Rhythm Patterns on page 6.)

4/4 Indicates that the basic rhythm will be 4 counts long, and that a quarter note will receive one full count.

| ♩ ♩ ♩ ♩ | Indicates that there are four regular beats of equal duration.

♪ Indicates a beat that is to be louder or heavier than normal.

160 Indicates there are to be 160 counts (in this notation it means drum beats as well) per minute.

AMERICAN INDIAN DANCES

Steps, Rhythms, Costumes, and Interpretation

1

Introduction

When most people think of Indians and dancing, they think of buckskin outfits, breechclouts, and headdresses, and a group of people jumping, raising their arms over their heads, shouting, and circling around a campfire. This was not so with the Indians. Their dances were unique and individual, according to the tribe and the purposes for which they were performed. It is hoped that through this book the dances of the American Indians will be shown forth in their true meaning and form. We are not saying that they are herein described exactly as the Indians danced them, for not even all Indians or different tribes danced the same dances exactly alike; but the dances as presented are, to our knowledge, in keeping with the true Indian spirit.

It is further hoped that readers of this book will be able to understand, teach, and perform these dances with the least possible difficulty, and present them with all the color, grace of movement, and meaning the Indians gave them. Certainly a culture so unique and colorful, which is today becoming lost by the tribes, and especially by their younger members, should be preserved. In a country great in historical heritage, no people contributed more to that heritage than the American Indian did out of his rich and colorful culture. The culture portrayed by his dances should be preserved. This is one of the primary purposes of this book.

Throughout every age, man has endeavored to express himself through the dance. Being no different from any other group in this respect, the American Indians developed dance movements typical of their way of life and their interpretation of it. Their dances were usually very serious expressions of important aspects of their lives, and were developed around their manner of living and their conception of such themes as hunting, fighting, farming, death, life, religion, medicine, and health.

Unlike the dances of the white man, Indian dances were generally danced by men only. Women usually entered into the occasion by forming a ring around the men dancers; and in unison with the drum or music,

3

they clapped their hands, chanted, or tapped their feet, swayed or balanced back and forth, and occasionally made comments encouraging the men dancers. Most tribes, however, developed a few social dances that were very popular with both men and women. These mixed dances were always danced in a social and recreational atmosphere. They laughed and teased, and very much enjoyed their social dances, and sometimes continued them for many hours at a time without changing or stopping the chanting. When a person or a couple tired, they would withdraw from the dance to rest for a short time, to re-enter the dance as they wished.

The typical Indian dance involves a single dancer or several participants who dance separately as their feelings move them; sometimes, as members of a group, they follow a set pattern of steps and mimic or follow a leader. Some of their dances are performed in lines or circles, with the dancers keeping in step with each other.

Traditionally, Indians danced in their central camp area or on any available open flat ground. Because they did not have smooth flat surfaces such as hardwood floors to dance upon, the Indians developed runs, jumps, hops, walks, balances, shuffles, stamps, and stomps, rather than sliding steps.

In many of their dances the Indians mimic animals, natural phenomena, and other men; in some they act out stories. When mimicking, they use graceful and intricate movements involving the entire body; this is especially noticeable in such beautiful dances as the Taos Horse Tail Dance and the Dance of the Dying Eagle. The Indians mimic with such vivid detail that observers can recognize the theme of a dance without difficulty; this is because Indians lived close to nature and depended upon their knowledge of it for their survival. Their close living with nature developed in them powers of observation that became the foundation upon which they developed many of their dances.

A distinguishing characteristic of Indian dancing is the way they extend the hand and arm in the direction of the forward foot and lean the head and body in the same direction. For example; as the right foot is placed forward or sideward, the right arm and hand are extended toward that foot and the head and body are also bent and turned in that direction. Another characteristic of their dancing is their use of bells and other noise makers while they dance. In many of their dances, Indians wear bells around their waists, arms, legs, and ankles and carry rattles which they shake in time with the drum, tom-tom, or chanted rhythm. The outfit of the Indian dancer is as important to him as the dance itself, and he takes great pride in being colorfully, neatly, and properly dressed.

General Information Concerning Presentation of the Dances

The dances are presented according to the following plan:

1. Title of the dance and indication as to the tribe or tribes that performed the dance.

2. An illustration of a dancer wearing the authentic outfit.

3. A brief story about the dance, covering the purpose of the dance, its theme, and some of the highlights of the action. This information is important and should be read carefully to obtain the proper understanding and feeling for what the dance is to portray.

4. A brief statement concerning the required outfit or outfits. Easy and inexpensive substitutions also are mentioned.

5. The procedure—a descriptive analysis, which refers to an illustrated pattern that is to be used as a guide, to supplement the description and simplify one's learning of the dances. Under this heading the parts of each dance are explained in numbered sections. The sections contain information concerning steps, basic drum beats, body positions, feelings to be portrayed by the dancer, starting position, number of dancers, etc. For example, in the Taos Horse Tail dance (Chap. 4), the first section reads:

1. The dancers line up in a straight line, one behind the other, at *A*. At the start of the drum beat, the dancers begin the Four-Beat Stomp (Chap. 3), drum beat 4/4 | ♩ ♩ ♩ ♪ | 180, and proceed forward to *B* (optional) . . . (etc.)

The Four-Beat Stomp is a basic dance step and is used in many of the Indian dances; because it is a basic step, the pattern is described in detail in Chapter 3, with other basic dance steps. It is suggested that persons using this book study and learn most of the basic steps before attempting the complete dances. Experience gained from teaching Indian dances has proven the advantages of proceeding in this manner.

The first section (as quoted above) includes the notation for the drum beat, or rhythm pattern, for the step. In this drum beat notation we see four quarter notes that indicate four drum beats, with the fourth beat receiving the accent and being louder or heavier than the other beats. Following the four drum beats is the number *180*. This figure represents the tempo or time of the beat, and indicates the number of times the quarter-note beat is repeated each minute.

The third section of the instructions for the Taos Horse Tail dance refers to a Toe-Heel-Chug step; and includes detailed directions for performing this step, because it is not among the basic steps covered—where the basic steps are called for, the reader is always referred to Chapter 3.

6. The pattern of the dance, presented in a simple illustration. Directional lines and figures of the Indian dancers show the steps and movements required in the various locations. Important positions in the pattern of the dance are designated or identified by letters *A, B, C*, etc., which are used in the detailed description of the dance procedure in referring to the illustration.

Rhythm Patterns

Most Indian rhythm patterns are chanted, drummed, or made by shaking rattles. The patterns are usually simple and composed of steady beats. However, the more complicated rhythm patterns involve drum rolls, rests, and short and long beats. To simplify the presentation of the rhythm patterns, standard musical notes, terms, and symbols are used. The following patterns are written for the drum but can be easily adapted to rattles.

1. 4/4 | ♩♩♩♩ | 160, an even drum pattern composed of four quarter notes. The numbers preceding the measure give the counts per measure and the kind of note that will equal one count. Here the *4/4* preceding the first bar denotes four counts to the measure, with the quarter notes to receive a full count each. All rhythm patterns are enclosed by bars. The number *160*, following the second bar, designates the tempo, or number of counts per minute.

2. 4/4 | ♩♩♩♩ | 180, a rhythm pattern composed of four even drum beats, with the first and third beats being accented. The tempo is 180 counts per minute.

3. 8/8 | ♩♩♪♪♪♪ | 120, a rhythm pattern composed of eight counts. The first two drum beats are quarter notes and therefore receive two counts each. The third, fourth, and fifth drum beats are eighth notes and receive one count each. The rest is an eighth rest and receives one count. The tempo is 120 counts per minute. This rhythm pattern can be found in the Buffalo Dance and is also the drum pattern of the Foot-and-Heel Shuffle basic dance step (Chap. 3).

4. 4/4 | ♩♩♩♩ | 160, an even drum pattern with each drum beat being accented and followed by a rest. This is a quarter rest and, therefore, it receives one count, the same as the drum beats. The tempo is 160 counts per minute.

5. 4/4 | ♩♩♩♩♩♩ | 160, a rhythm pattern for a drum roll composed of three quick beats, followed by a quarter rest sign. Each drum roll and each rest is given one full count. The tempo is 160 counts per minute.

In different tribes and locations, many of the dances that are supposed to be the same vary as to pattern, rhythm, and step and the number and sex of the dancers. In some of the explanations of the dances important variations are mentioned; but for the most part, to facilitate the learning of the dances for the beginner, many of their more complicated variations have been omitted purposely, only the simpler and more popular patterns being included in this introductory book. The number following each rhythm pattern designates the maximum tempo at which the step is usually danced. During the learning of the dance, and the step and for inexperienced dancers, the drum beat may be slower than indicated.

Meanings of Symbols and Terms

L and *R* are used to designate left or right when referring to a part of the body, as in "the L leg is moved sideward." This designation is used only when referring to an arm, leg, hand, or foot. Sometimes for clarity, the words *left* and *right* are spelled out. Following is a list of symbols used in the illustrations of the dance steps.

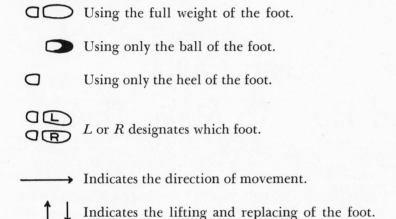

Using the full weight of the foot.

Using only the ball of the foot.

Using only the heel of the foot.

L or *R* designates which foot.

⟶ Indicates the direction of movement.

↑ ↓ Indicates the lifting and replacing of the foot.

2

Indian Outfits
and How To Make Them

For outfits to be truly Indian they must be designed and decorated properly. In this chapter, the parts of each outfit are carefully illustrated and explained for the purpose of helping leaders who are interested in making their own outfits. The outfits described resemble as much as possible the true Indian shape, color, and design. The genuine materials used by the Indians are discussed. Inexpensive substitute materials, geared more closely to the need of the layman and other inexperienced participants, are mentioned. This chapter also contains a section showing many Indian designs that might be used when decorating outfits, scenery, or stage backgrounds and props. The designs are identified as to tribe or general area to help readers make proper selections. When decorating, it is best to use the designs of one tribe or area and not combine or mix them.

Most Indians used stenciling, painting, bead work, and fringe in making their decorations. Especially did they use bead work on leather, but for practical purposes the designs can be painted upon the leather outfits. When using corduroy or similar substitute materials, designs can be cut from colored felt and sewed onto the material.

Indians also decorated many of their outfits with fringe. The articles usually decorated with fringe were boleros, cuffs, breechclouts, war shirts, and leggings. Fringe adds to the authenticity and beauty of many Indian outfits and should be added for effectiveness.

The various parts of the Indian outfits are conveniently arranged and presented in alphabetical order. Explanations are brief and the illustrations have been purposely kept simple, easy to follow, relatively complete, and authentic.

Along with each dance presented in this book is shown the complete

Indian outfit or outfits needed. Indian figures are shown properly wearing the outfits. The parts of each outfit are listed, and readers have only to refer to this chapter to learn how to make them. It is hoped that, in presenting the outfits for each dance, another aspect of Indian culture will be appreciated and preserved.

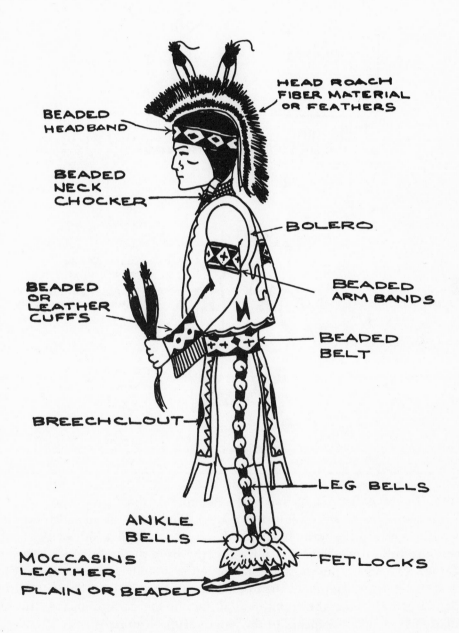

BRAVE WEARING STANDARD OUTFIT

BOLERO

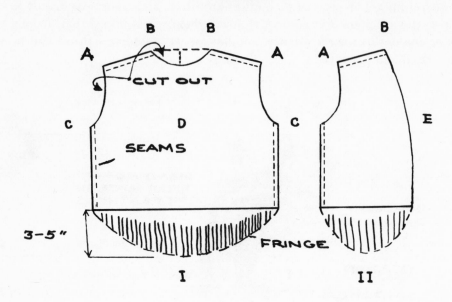

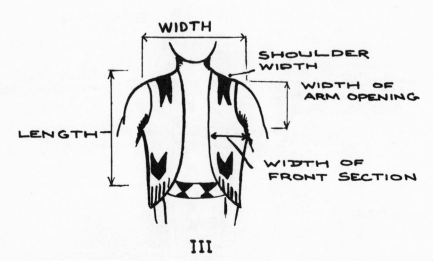

1. To make the back section of the bolero, first draw the desired pattern upon a sheet of paper, such as newspaper. To obtain the length, measure from B down to the waist line. To determine the full width of the back, measure from under one arm pit across the back to the opposite arm pit, C to C. To obtain the width of the top of the shoulder, measure from A to B. Also, measure and mark the distance from A to A, the shoulder width—Figs. I and III. For the seams, add ½ inch to the measurements. If you desire fringe, add 3–5 inches to the length of the pattern.

2. To make the neck opening, first obtain the size of the neck and mark the two points *B*. From the center of the distance from *B* to *B*, measure down 2 inches, and make a pencil mark. Draw a curving neckline from *B* to *B* through this pencil mark. Cut out along this line—Fig. I.

3. To determine the size of the arm opening, measure from *A*, the tip of the shoulder, to the center of the arm pit, *C*. When cutting out this opening, make it 1 inch bigger if you desire a loose fit—Figs. I and III.

4. The front pieces use the same length measurements as the back piece. The full width of each side section should be the distance from *C* to *E*, from under the arm to the center of the chest—Figs. II and III. Cut the top of the front sections from *A* to *B* to match the corresponding parts of the back section. Be sure to leave ½ inch at top and side for seams and the extra length for the fringe—Fig. II. The arm openings should be made to match those in the back section. When you have completed one front section turn it over and trace it upon another piece of paper. This is the other side of the pattern. Pin the pattern together and place it upon the wearer. Adjust and make any necessary changes in the pattern. Place the pattern upon the material and cut out the sections. Sew them together, and with scissors, make the fringe.

Make the bolero from buckskin, soft leather, heavy felt, corduroy or any heavy brightly colored material. Decorate the bolero with painted designs, colored felt, or bead work.

BANDS—ARM, HEAD, OR LEG

LOOM BEADED

I

1. Arm, head, and leg bands are generally beaded. They are usually made on a bead loom—Fig. I.

2. If loomed beadwork is unavailable or impractical, sew brightly col-

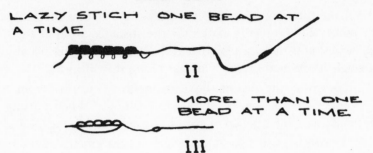

ored beads upon a felt or soft leather band. Use the lazy stitch as shown in Figs. II and III.

Bands can also be made by sewing colored felt designs upon the band. Designs can be made upon soft leather with paint.

BELLS—ANKLE

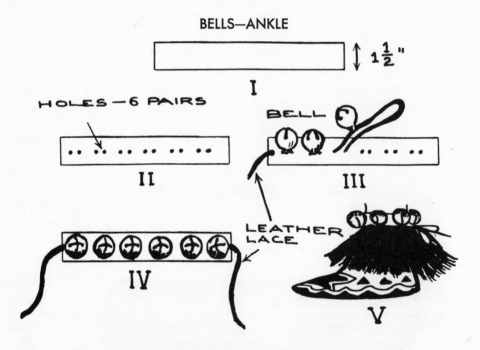

1. Cut from a piece of cowhide a band 1½ inches wide, and long enough to fit around the ankle—Fig. I.

2. Punch 6 pair of holes evenly spaced around the band—Fig. II.

3. Run a leather lace through the holes and place a small metal bell on the lace at each pair of holes—Figs. III and IV.

4. Leave about 5 inches of the lace at each end of the band for tying the bells securely around the ankle—Figs. IV and V.

Shoelaces may be used for lacing. An old leather belt can be substituted for the cowhide strip.

BELLS—LEG

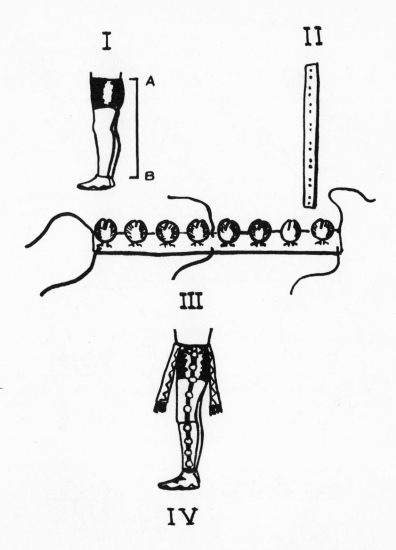

1. From leather cut out a strip 1½ inches wide and in length the distance from A to B—Fig. I.

2. Using the same methods as in the directions for making the ankle bell band, fasten the bells to the long leg band—Figs. II and III.

3. Punch holes at the ends and center of the strip and lace the tying strips in place. Notice that the tying laces fasten at the waist, the ankle, and slightly above or below the knee—Figs. III and IV.

A heavy plastic or felt material can be substituted for the band. Shoe laces can be used for the tying strings instead of leather strips.

BONNET—WAR OR FEATHERED

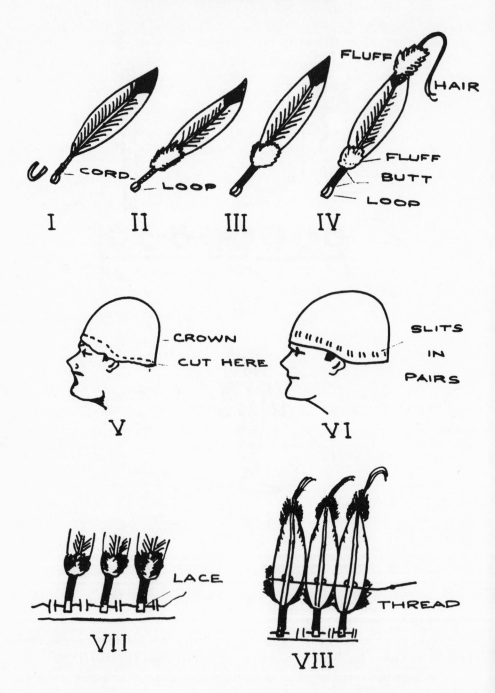

1. An average sized bonnet requires thirty feathers. The feathers should be large and of a uniform type and size. Wing and tail feathers of hawk, eagle, or turkey are best for this purpose. Strip the hair or fuzz from the butt or end of the quills. Fold a piece of leather or plastic ¼ inch wide and 4 inches long and bind it to the butt of the quill—Fig. I. Use thread or twine to bind the leather loop to the bottom of the quill. Be sure to leave the small loop of leather protruding below the end of the feather. The loop should be placed parallel to the vane of the feather.

2. Place several fluffy feathers together and glue them to the base of the feather. Also, be sure the fluff is glued to the top side of the feather. The top side is curved and is the shiny side—Fig. II.

3. Wrap a strip of brightly colored felt around the butt of the feather. It should cover the binding and also the ends of the fluff feathers—Fig. III.

4. With glue, fasten tip fluff and hair to the top end of the feather— Fig. IV.

5. Cut the brim from an old felt hat, mark the crown as in Fig. V, and trim the crown along markings.

6. Cut thirty pairs of slits in crown—Fig. VI. Slits should be about ¼ inch long, and the two slits of a pair about ¼ inch apart. The spacing from one pair to the next should vary according to the size of the crown.

7. Using a long cord or narrow leather strip, fasten or sew each feather in position—Fig. VII.

8. To hold the feathers together and to prevent slipping and crossing, sew them together with a needle and strong thread. When pushing the needle through the quill, do not bend the quill or weaken it. The sewing is done on the back side of the feather and behind the fluff—Figs. VIII and IX.

9. Decorate the front section of the finished bonnet with paint, beadwork or pieces of brightly colored felt—Fig. X.

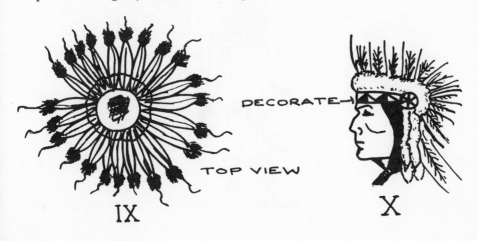

DECORATE

TOP VIEW

IX   X

BREECHCLOUT

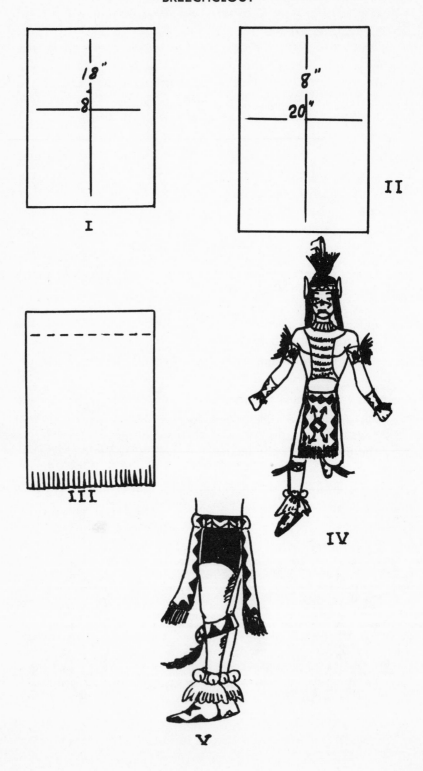

1. Cut two pieces of material 8 inches wide and 18 inches long; if you want fringe along the bottom of the material, increase the length to 20 inches—Figs. I and II.

2. Along the top edge, loop the material over about 2 inches and sew in place—Fig. III. The costume's belt fits in this loop.

3. With scissors, fringe the bottom edge of the sections—Fig. III.

The front view of the breechclout, showing decorations and how it is worn is illustrated in Fig. IV; the side view, showing position of the belt, is illustrated in Fig. V.

BUSTLE—FEATHERED

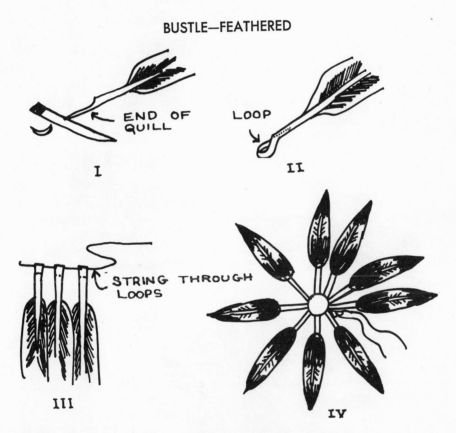

1. Shave or cut the end of the quill—Fig. I.

2. Bend the slender shaved quill end into a loop and slide the tip end of the quill into the hollow part of the quill—Fig. II.

3. Thread the feathers on a cord by running the cord through each loop—Fig. III.

4. After all the feathers have been placed on the cord tie the ends of the cord together; pull the string tightly to form the feathers into a circle—Fig. IV.

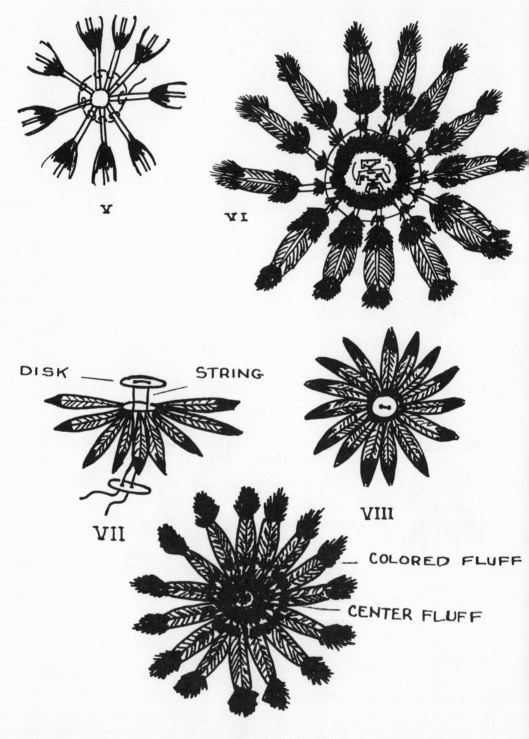

V

VI

DISK   STRING

VII

VIII

COLORED FLUFF

CENTER FLUFF

IX

5. Run needle and thread through and around each feather—Fig. V; this holds the feathers in their circle position—Fig. VI.

6. Lace together two leather disks, and place at top and bottom or on each side of the bustle—Fig. VII. (Disks can be made from heavy cardboard, wood, tin, or bone, if leather is not available.) Tighten the thread holding the feathers and make the circle of feathers smaller than the size of the disks.

7. Bring the disks togther by pulling the strings and tying their ends together—Fig. VIII.

8. Cover the center disk with fluff, and tip each feather with brightly colored fluff—Fig. IX.

CUFFS

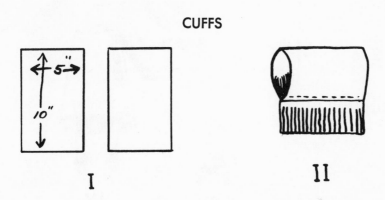

I   II

III

1. To make two cuffs, cut out two pieces of material 5 inches wide and 10 inches long; if you wish fringe, increase the length by about 2 inches—Figs. I and II.

2. Loop the material over and sew in place. With scissors, clip the fringe—Figs. II and III.

3. Decorate the cuffs with beadwork or painted designs—Fig. III.

Cuffs can be made of felt, flannel, soft leather, or any type of heavy material. Completed cuff is shown in correct position on the arm.

DRESS—SQUAW

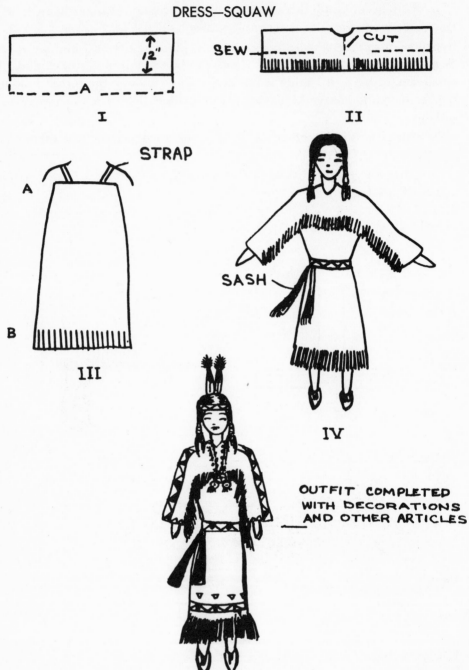

1. With arms outstretched, take the measurement from wrist to wrist, *A*. This is the length of the shoulder cape. Cut out from your material a cape 24 inches wide and fold it—Fig. I.

2. Measure the length of the arm, mark this distance upon the folded material, and sew from the edge of the material over to the mark to form the sleeve—Fig. II.

3. Cut out a curving neckline, and at the center of the neckline on the back section of the cape make a 2-inch cut—Fig. II. Fringe the back and front sections of the cape with scissors.

4. To obtain the length of the skirt, measure from *A* (armpit) down to about 10 inches from the ground. Skirt can be made as full as wanted. Turn the material inside out and sew together at the side. Run a seam along the top edge of the skirt and put a draw cord or an elastic band through it. This will hold the skirt to the body. Sew two shoulder straps to the top of the skirt, and fringe the bottom of the skirt—Fig. III.

5. To decorate the dress sew on beadwork or felt designs, or paint with bright designs. Tie a sash around the waist.

Figure IV shows the proper way to wear the woman's outfit. Women also wear a headband with one or two feathers tucked in at the rear of the head, moccasins, bracelets, rings, and necklaces.

FETLOCKS

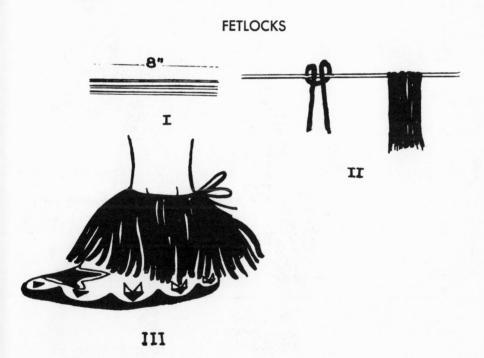

1. Cut yarn or heavy string into 8-inch strips—Fig. I.

2. Loop the yarn over a shoelace or string—Fig. II. The shoelace should be long enough to reach around the ankle and have sufficient length for tying. After the yarn has been looped on the lace, grasp the two ends of the yarn and pull to tighten it securely to the lace, and push each looped strand tightly against the others.

Completed fetlock, showing lace closely covered with yarn and tied properly around the ankle, is illustrated in Fig. III.

LEGGINGS

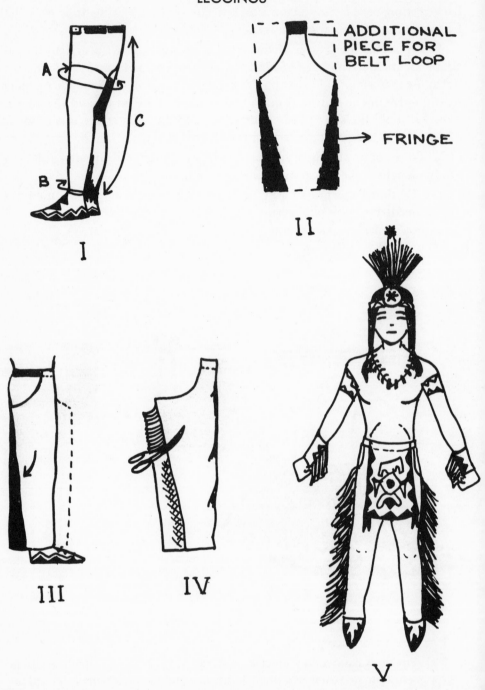

1. At *A* measure the leg—Fig. I. At *B* measure the ankle. Increase these measurements for a seam and any fringe desired. To determine length, measure *C*, the distance from the ankle to the waistline, and add 3 inches for the belt loop.

2. Mark and cut out the pattern—Fig. II. Use the measurements *A*, *B*, and *C*. The shaded area indicates fringe.

3. Fold the legging and sew—Fig. III.

4. Fringe the additional side material—Fig. IV.

Figure V shows the proper way to wear the leggings; note also the position of the breechclout. Leggings can be made from buckskin, felt, flannel, canvas, or almost any type of heavy material.

MOCCASINS

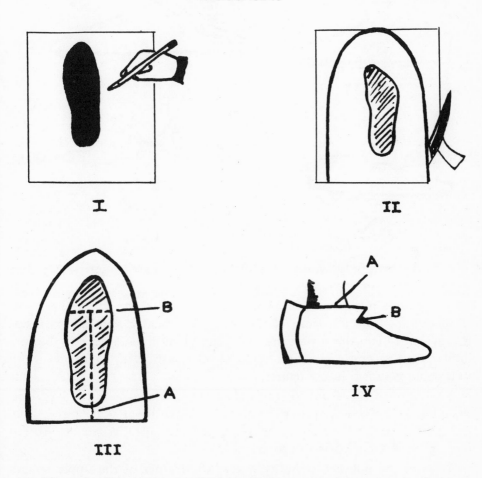

1. Place the foot upon a piece of paper and trace the outline—Fig. I; this is the pattern for the sole of the moccasin. Turn this pattern over and retrace for the opposite foot. From medium heavy leather, cut out the soles.

2. On paper, draw another pattern of the outline of the foot—Fig. II. This is the pattern of the top part of the moccasin. Cut it out, Fig. III,

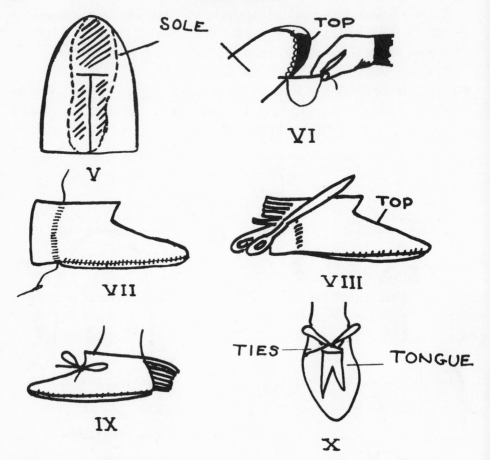

leaving the margin as shown; make the paper upper section larger than necessary and trim it later as necessary.

3. On the top section of the pattern, mark lines *A* and *B*. The distance of these lines from the front of the pattern is usually 4 inches; however, this depends upon the size of the foot. Cut along lines *A* and *B*. Be sure to make this pattern with about the same relationships in length and width to the sole as shown in the figure.

4. Fold open the *A* and *B* cuts and place the foot inside the upper section—Fig. IV. Trim the pattern as necessary; leave about ½ inch folded under the foot for the overlap on which to sew the sole. When the pattern fits, cut out leather parts to match.

5. Turn the polished or shiny side of the leather of the upper section inside and place it over the shiny side of the sole; the two edges come together flat at heel and toe—Fig. V. Start at the toe of the moccasin and sew the sole and the top together, edge to edge (do not fold the edge of the upper section)—Fig. VI.

6. After the sole has been completely sewed to the upper section, turn the moccasin right side out and then sew up the back or rear section of the boot; leave the extra leather for the fringe—Fig. VII.

7. With scissors, fringe the additional leather on the back of the mocassin —Figs. VIII and IX.

8. Cut out and sew in place a leather tongue, and on each side of the shoe sew a tie string—Fig. X.

Use soft leather or buckskin for the uppers and a heavy or medium heavy leather for the soles.

RATTLES

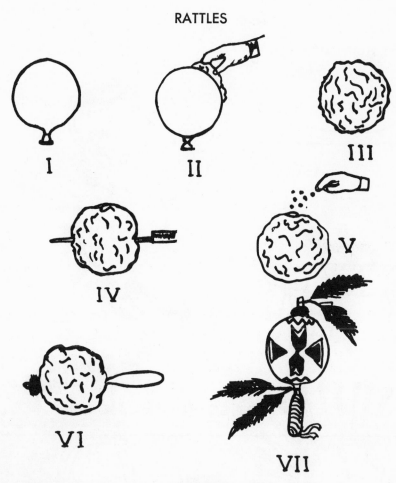

1. Inflate a medium sized rubber balloon and cover it with papier-mâché—Figs. I, II, and III. Allow the papier-mâché to dry thoroughly before continuing the project.

2. After the papier-mâché is dry, punch holes in each end with a sharp instrument and break the balloon—Fig. IV.

3. Through one of the openings, insert small rocks, seeds or sand—Fig. V.

4. Place a stick through the rattle; it should extend 2 inches above and

about 8 inches below the rattle—Fig. VI. To keep the stick in place, wrap the top end with tape, cord or felt.

5. Paint the rattle with Indian designs and tie feathers or colored fluff to the stick—Fig. VII.

Gourds, old milk cans, or small cardboard boxes can be used in place of the rubber ballon.

ROACH—FEATHERED

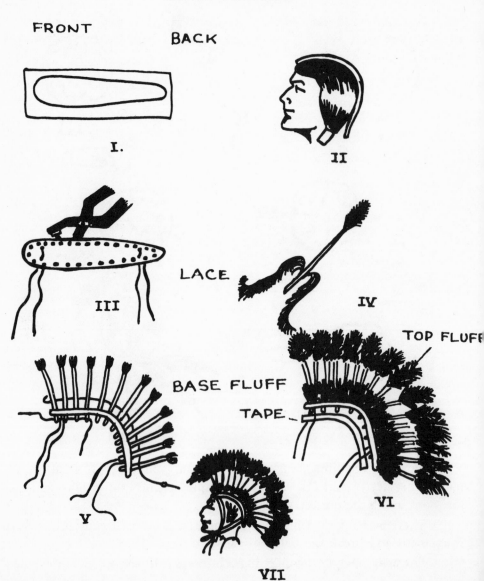

1. Cut out a piece of medium heavy leather into a section 2 inches wide and 10 inches long, tapering slightly at one end, as in Fig. I. The strip of leather fits on the brave's head, as shown in Fig. II.

2. Punch holes evenly around the edge of the headpiece—Fig. III. Near the front and back ends of the top piece, punch two additional holes for each of the tie strings.

3. With thumb and forefinger, strip the hair from two thirds of each feather, leaving the hair at the top—Fig. IV. Prepare as many feathers as you have holes in the headpiece.

4. Poke the ends of the feathers through the holes in the leather, and with a needle and thread run a thread through the quills of the feathers, tying them together below the leather piece; and then run a thread through the quills above the leather—Fig. V.

5. Glue feather fluffs on the base and tip of each feather—Fig. VI. Place a strip of adhesive tape over the quill ends.

Figure VII shows the completed roach and the method of holding it on the head. Note the tie strings tied under the chin. The top piece can be made from cowhide, a leather belt or any stiff leather. Fluff is the light fluffy feathers found under a bird's tail; it is light and downy and can be painted or dyed different colors.

ROACH—HAIR OR FIBER

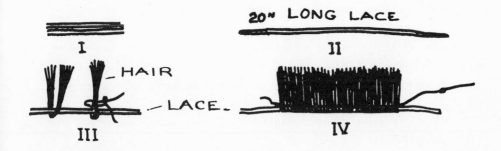

1. Cut rope fiber, horse-tail hair, porcupine hair or other coarse animal hair into 10-inch strips—Fig. I.

2. Bend the sections of hair over a leather lace (Fig. II), and fasten them in place with a strong thread or cord, tying each section of hair in place with a slip knot or whip stitch and pushing the hair sections tightly against each other—Figs. III and IV. Each group or section of hair should be composed of enough hair to make a bundle about ¼ inch in diameter.

3. Place the length of fiber flat down on a hard surface, and with a tooth

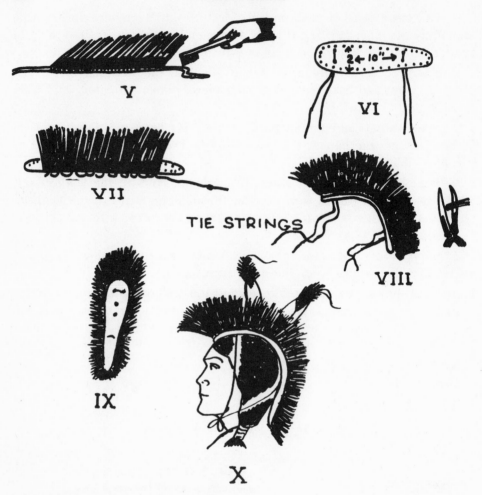

brush, dye it with colored ink—Fig. V. If you are using porcupine hair leave it in its natural color.

4. From medium heavy leather cut out a foundation head piece—Fig. VI. (Refer to Directions 1 and 2 for the Feather Roach.)

5. Place the string of fiber around the leather piece and sew it in place with heavy thread—Fig. VII.

6. With scissors, trim the fiber; make it 5 inches high in front and 3 inches in the back—Figs. VIII and IX. Use a stiff comb to smooth and straighten hair.

Figure X shows the Roach in proper wearing position.

SHIRT—WAR

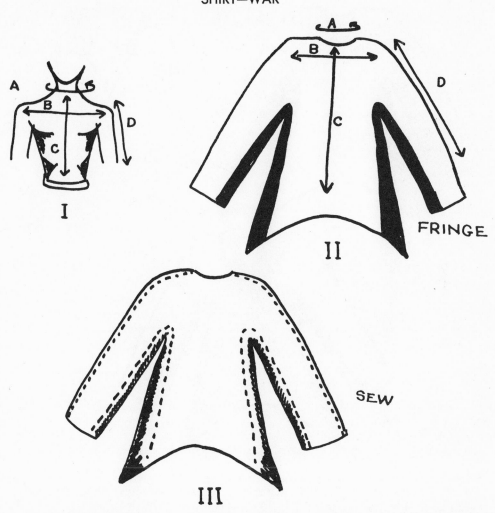

1. To determine the measurements for the war shirt, measure the neck, chest, torso and arm, at *A, B, C,* and *D*—Fig. I. Make the shirt roomy and allow extra length and width for hemming. Under the arms and sides of the shirt allow ½ inch to 3 inches for fringe (shaded area)—Fig. II.

2. Draw the pattern on a large piece of paper. Cut out two identical patterns of the shirt and pin them together. Place the paper shirt on the person and make any necessary adjustments. After the adjustments have been made, cut out the shirt from your material and sew it together, as shown in Fig. III.

3. Fringe the shaded area—Fig. IV.

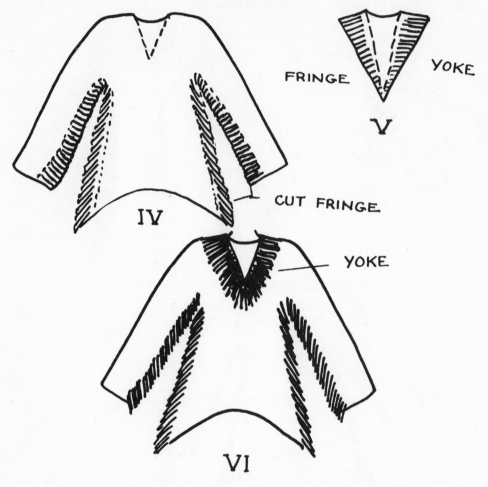

4. From another piece of material, cut out a fringed V shaped neck yoke—Fig. V. Sew the yoke in position around the neck—Fig. VI.

Use soft leather, buckskin, felt, flannel, or corduroy. The shirt can be decorated with painted designs, beadwork, or pieces of colored felt.

YOKE

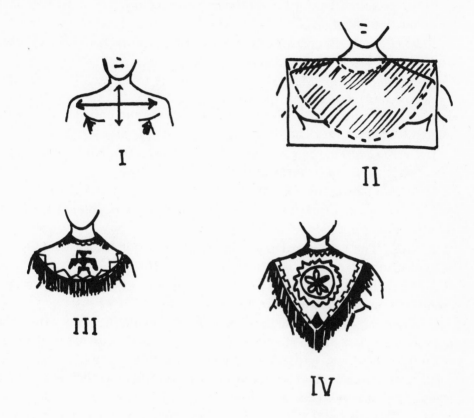

I

II

III

IV

1. Measure the width from shoulder tip to shoulder tip, and the length from neckline to sternum—Fig. I.

2. Fold a piece of paper and cut it to the desired length and width, and then determine the neck opening and cut it out—Fig. II. Place the paper yoke on the person and make the necessary adjustments. If you desire fringe, leave about three inches for this purpose.

3. From yoke material, cut out the desired pattern—Figs. III and IV. The shape of the yoke can vary according to your wishes.

A yoke can be made from soft leather, felt, velvet, or any type of heavy material.

MISCELLANEOUS PIECES OF OUTFITS AND INFORMATION

1. *Fur pieces.* Strips of fur can be cut from tanned rabbit skin, ¾ inch wide and 10 inches long.

2. *Body paint.* Regular grease paint can be used, or paint can be made from mixing soap and poster paint.

3. *Bow and arrow.* Make the arrow from any round stick or a commercial arrow can be used with the point changed. Make an arrowhead from wood or cardboard. Buy a commercial bow of simple construction, and tie colored feathers at each end of the bow.

4. *Deer headdress.* Sew brown fur to the crown of an old felt hat. With wire, mount small deer horns to the sides of the crown.

5. *Buffalo headdress.* Mount cow horns to a fur covered felt crown.

6. *Under garment.* Swim trunks, gym pants, or dark colored tights can be worn under outfits.

7. *Sash.* The sash is used as a belt and can be made from a long piece of colored material.

8. *Tunic* or *Skirt.* A large piece of canvas, felt, or corduroy is wrapped around the waist and worn like a skirt.

9. *Eagle wings.* Eagle wings are made by mounting or sewing large feathers upon a 12-inch-wide piece of heavy material. The material should reach from one wrist, across the shoulder, to the other wrist.

10. *Dance wand.* The wand can be made by tying together with cord or leather the butt ends of two feathers.

11. *Feathered headband.* A piece of heavy material about 1 inch wide is used to place around the head. It can be decorated with paint, felt, or beads. Sew one or two feathers at the back of the headband.

12. *Horsetail.* This is made from the hair of a horse's tail or from black, white, or brown yarn.

13. *Old Man's Mask.* This can be made by applying papier-mâché to wire mesh or upon a large ice cream carton.

14. *Coup stick.* Sew feathers on a piece of material 8 inches wide and about 4 feet long and apply to a stick about the length of a broom stick.

15. *Zuni Rain Dance mask.* This can be made from a 1- or 2-gallon cardboard ice cream container.

16. *Shield.* The shield can be made with Masonite, or heavy cardboard. Decorate with designs and fasten feathers to its edges so that they hang downward.

17. *Quills.* These are the feathers that generally come from the wing or tail of the bird, usually the largest, and can be used for bonnets, bustles, headdresses, etc.—Fig. I.

I

FLUFF

II

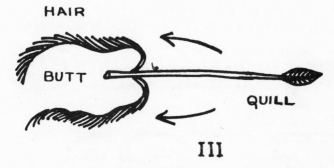

III

18. *Fluff.* This is the down or fluffy feathers generally found under a bird's tail feathers—Fig. II.

19. *To strip a quill,* take each side of a feather and, with thumb and forefinger, strip off or remove part of the hair and fuzz, leaving part of the quill bare or without hair—Fig. III.

BASIC INDIAN DESIGNS

Apache

Northwest

Eastern and Southeastern Woodland

Navajo

Yuma

3

Basic Indian Dance Steps

American Indian dancers developed several basic dance steps which became popular among most of the Indian tribes of America. Even though individual Indian tribes produced dance steps that were performed only by their own respective groups, they generally used the basic steps used by most other tribes. This condition did not hold true of dances that portrayed or mimicked. In these dances, the Indians broke away from the traditional basic steps and employed foot and body actions resembling the bird, animal, or whatever creature they were depicting.

In this chapter are presented the dance steps that are basic to many Indian dances. Throughout the book, the non-basic steps are described in the procedures pertaining to each dance, whereas readers are referred to this chapter for the basic steps.

STANDARD STARTING POSITION

1. The dancer stands with his body weight on his L foot. The R knee is bent, allowing the toe or ball of the R foot to touch the ground about even with the arch of the L foot.

2. For some of the dances the arm and body positions vary, but their usual positions are as follows. The R arm is bent at the elbow and the hand is approximately even with the toe of the R foot. The L arm is usually held in the same relative position except that it is somtimes held higher than the right and with the hand closer to the dancer's body. In this position the R arm is easily moved forward as the R foot makes the first step. This particular movement is typical of most Indian dances. The arms, hands, and head often follow the direction taken by the foot movements.

STANDARD STARTING POSITION

3. The body position is usually erect or slightly bent forward from the hips.

The above described standard starting position is the starting position for most of the steps used in this book. All variations of this position are described in the procedures for the particular dances.

ONE-FOOT STOMP

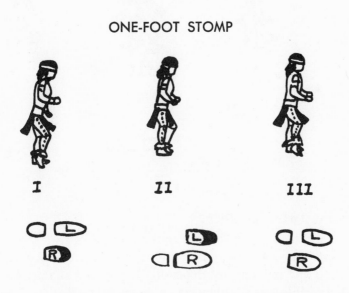

1. Standard starting position, but with the toe of the R foot even with or slightly behind the left heel—Fig. I.

2. For this step, the drum beat consists of four steady beats with the first and third beats accented. 4/4 | ♪ ♪ ♪ ♪ | 160 to 180. Tempo is 160 to 180 counts per minute depending upon the characteristics of the dance.

3. On beat one, the knee of the R leg is straightened and the foot is shoved forward a few inches, but not ahead of the L foot. Simultaneously with this forward action, strike the heel of the R foot sharply against the ground and shift the body weight from the left to the right foot. As the weight of the body is shifted, raise the heel of the L foot from the ground—Fig. II.

4. On beat two, the knee of the L leg is straightened and the L foot is moved forward without a heel stomp, and placed upon the ground about eight inches ahead of the R foot. Note that in this step the L foot is always ahead of the R foot—Figs. II and III. However, it is permissible to lead with the R foot. When using this variation, do not change the actions of the right or left foot. The only variation is in the relative position of the feet.

At the finish of the above action, the dancer should be in the starting position and ready to repeat the above action on beats three and four.

HEEL-TOE STEP

1. Standard starting position.

2. The drum beat for this step is four steady beats with the accent upon beats two and four. 4/4 | ♩ ♩̂ ♩ ♩̂ | 140–160. The tempo may vary from 140 to 160 counts per minute depending upon the characteristics of the dance and the ability of the dancers.

3. On beat one, the dancer steps diagonally forward, placing his R heel upon the ground. The head, hand, and body movements follow the foot actions; as the R foot is moved forward, the body leans, the head turns and the hand is extended in the direction of the foot—Fig. I.

4. On beat two, the toe of the R foot is sharply lowered to the ground, shifting the body weight to the R foot; simultaneously, the L knee is bent, raising the L heel or entire foot, if desired—Fig. II.

5. On drum beats three and four, repeat directions 3 and 4 for opposite foot and body actions—Figs. III and IV.

When performing this step the dancer changes his line of direction by placing his feet in the direction he desires to go. Cross-over steps are also permissible.

TOE-HEEL STEP

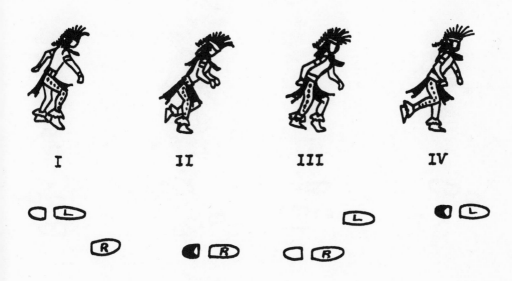

1. Standard starting position.

2. The drum beat for this step is four steady beats with the accent upon the first and third beats. 4/4 | ♪ ♩ ♪ ♩ | 140–160. The tempo may vary from 140 to 160 counts per minute depending upon the characteristics of the dance and the ability of the dancers.

3. On beat one, the dancer steps forward or diagonally forward with his R leg and places the toe of his foot on the ground—Fig. I. Remember the body and hand actions follow the foot actions. The R hand is moved forward as the R leg is extended.

4. On beat two, the R heel is sharply lowered to the ground, shifting the entire body weight to the R foot—Fig. II. Simultaneously, the L knee is bent, raising the L heel or the entire foot off the ground. The L hand action is in the direction of the L foot action.

5. On drum beats three and four, repeat the above directions for opposite foot and hand movements—Figs. III and IV.

While using this step the dancer can travel in any direction desired. It is a very good step to use when backing up.

HEEL SHUFFLE

1. Standard starting position.

2. The drum beat for this step is four steady beats. 4/4 | ♩♩♩♩ | 140–160. The tempo may vary from 140 to 160 counts per minute depending upon the characteristics of the dance and the ability of the dancers.

3. On beat one, the dancer extends his R leg diagonally forward about 12 inches and places his R heel upon the ground—Fig. I. The body and arm actions follow the foot movement with the R arm being extended toward the R foot.

4. On drum beat two, the dancer slides the R heel backward about six inches and at the same time, without raising the heel, sharply strikes the ball of his R foot flat upon the ground—Fig. II. Simultaneously with this backward action the L heel is raised and the foot is drawn backward a few inches. The weight is shifted from the L to R foot. In this action the entire body moves backward. The action is best described as a sliding backward hop or shuffle.

5. On drum beats three and four, repeat the above described shuffle with opposite foot, hand, and body movements—Figs. III and IV.

This is an easy step to master once a person can do the toe-heel step. The only difference is the backward hop slide or shuffle. The dancer when using this step usually weaves and pivots and turns from side to side while progressing forward and around the dance area.

FOOT-AND-HEEL SHUFFLE

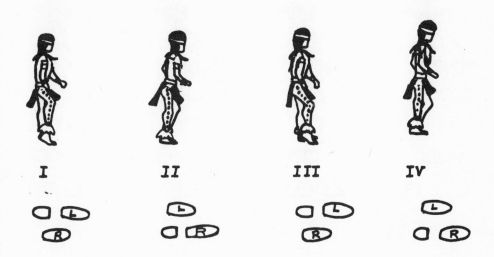

I   II   III   IV

1. Standard starting position.

2. The drum beat for this step starts with two slow, heavy beats of 2 counts each; then come three fast beats, followed by an eighth rest. 8/8 | ♩ ♩ ♪ ♪ ♪₇ | 120. Tempo is 120 counts per minute.

3. On the first long drum beat, the dancer shoves the ball of his R foot forward from 6 to 8 inches, with his weight over it, and at the same time sharply strikes his R heel to the ground; during this stomp action, the L knee is bent and the L heel is raised as the body weight is shifted to the R foot, and the R arm, head, and body move in the direction of the working or R foot—Figs I and II.

4. On the second long drum beat the dancer shoves his L foot forward 6 to 8 inches, with his weight over it, and simultaneously strikes his L heel to the ground; during this action he bends his R knee and shifts his weight to his L foot, his body and arm actions following the foot actions—Fig. III.

5. On the quick drum beats, three, four, and five, the dancer repeats the ball-heel shuffle, using alternate footwork; first the right foot, then the left, and then the right foot again. These three steps are performed relatively fast. At the completion of the fifth step the R foot is upon the ground with the weight of the body upon this foot—Fig. IV. The L knee is bent and the dancer is in position to repeat the five shuffle steps starting with the L foot. (Notice the short rest before repeating the five shuffle steps.)

FOUR-BEAT STOMP

1. Standard starting position.

2. The drum beat for this step is four steady beats, with the last or fourth beat receiving an accent. 4/4 | ♩ ♩ ♩ ♩̂ | 140–180. The tempo may vary from 140 to 180 counts per minute depending upon the characteristics of the dance and the ability of the dancers.

3. On beat one, the dancer performs a low hop on his L foot which carries him forward approximately six inches, at the same time extending his R leg forward and tapping his R toe upon the ground—Fig. I. The hand and body actions are in the direction of the R foot.

4. On beats two and three, with the R foot remaining extended forward, the dancer repeats the low forward hopping on his L foot and the tapping of the R toe—Fig. I.

5. On beat four, the dancer hops backward on his L foot about 12 inches, at the same time bringing his R foot back into a position slightly ahead of or even with, the toes of his L foot—Fig. II. As he completes the backward movement, the dancer transfers his weight to his R foot. The dancer is now in position to repeat the above described movements using opposite foot and body actions—Figs. III and IV.

WAR DANCE STEP

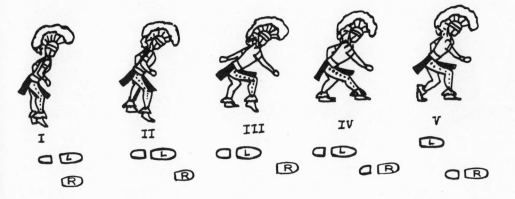

1. Standard starting position.

2. In this step the drum beat is four steady beats with the last or fourth beat receiving an accent. 4/4 | ♩ ♩ ♩ ♩̂ | 120. Tempo is 120 counts per minute.

3. On beat one the dancer taps the toe of his R foot upon the ground slightly ahead of or even with the L foot—Fig. I. Do not move the L foot.

4. On beat two, the dancer moves his R foot forward about 3 inches ahead of the first tap and again taps his toe upon the ground—Fig. II.

5. On beat three he again extends his foot forward a few inches and repeats the tap—Fig. III.

6. On the fourth beat, the dancer steps forward with his R foot and places it flat upon the ground. The R knee is almost straight. He then rocks forward, as in walking, and shifts his body weight to the R foot, simultaneously lifting his L heel—Figs. IV and V. The dancer is now in position to repeat the pattern with the opposite foot.

When performing this step it is also permissible for the dancer to pivot on the stationary foot towards the tapping foot.

WAR DANCE STEP—VARIATION

1. Standard starting position.

2. The drum beat for this step is three medium loud steady beats and then one heavy beat. $4/4$ | ♩ ♩ ♩ ♪ | 120–160. The tempo may vary from 120 to 160 counts per minute depending upon the characteristics of the dance and the ability of the dancers.

3. On beat one, the dancer makes a low hop in place on his L foot and at the same time extends his R foot slightly forward and taps his R toe upon the ground—Fig. I.

4. On beat two, the dancer repeats the low hop on the L foot and R toe tap; the toe tap is made about 3 inches ahead of the position of the first tap—Fig. II.

5. On beat three, the dancer repeats the low hop on his L foot and taps his R heel upon the ground; the heel tap is made about 3 inches ahead of the previous toe tap—Fig. III.

6. On beat four, the dancer again hops upon his L foot and at the same time places his complete R foot upon the ground about one foot ahead of the L foot—Fig. IV. As the R foot touches the ground the dancer leans or rocks forward on his R foot and also shifts his body weight forward to his R foot. As the body weight is shifted, the dancer raises the heel of his L foot, and this action puts him in position to repeat the dance step using opposite foot actions—Fig. V.

CANOE STEP

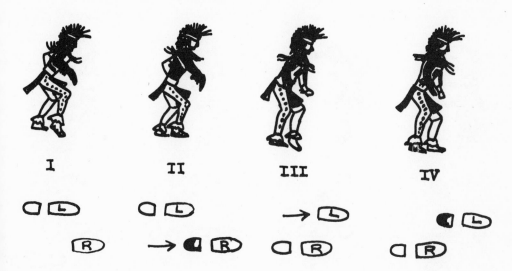

1. Standard starting position.

2. The drum beat for this step is four steady beats with the second and fourth beats accented, and heavier than beats one and three. 4/4 | ♩♩♩♩ | 160. The tempo is 160 counts per minute.

3. On beat one, the dancer extends his R foot diagonally forward and places his R toe upon the ground—Fig. I.

4. On beat two, the R toe is slipped or shuffled forward a few inches and at the same time the R heel is snapped or stomped sharply upon the ground—Fig. II. During this action the weight of the body is shifted to the R foot. Notice that both feet are flat upon the ground.

5. On beats three and four, repeat the above for opposite footwork.

CROSS-OVER STI-YU

1. Standard starting position.

2. The drum beat for this step is three medium loud but steady beats and then one heavy beat. 4/4 | ♩ ♩ ♩ ♪ | 120–160. The tempo may vary from 120 to 160 counts per minute depending upon the characteristics of the dance and the ability of the dancers.

3. On beat one, the dancer makes a low hop in place upon his L foot, at the same time extending his R foot diagonally forward a few inches and tapping his R toe upon the ground—Fig. I.

4. On beat two, the dancer repeats the low hop on his L foot; at the same time he bends his R knee and crosses his R leg over his L leg and taps his R toe upon the ground at the left side of his L foot—Fig. II.

5. On beat three, the dancer repeats the low hop on his L foot. He extends his R leg and taps his R toe in front of his body—Fig. III.

6. On beat four, the dancer repeats the low hop on his L foot. He extends his R leg straight forward placing his complete foot flat upon the ground—Fig. IV. He immediately rocks forward on his forward foot and shifts the weight of his body to it. The dancer is now in position to continue the dance step with opposite footwork.

Sti-yu is pronounced stē-ya. Its meaning is to extend knee or thrust foot outward.

PAWING STEP

I   II   III

1. Starting position: The dancer stands in an erect position with his feet together and with the weight of the body on the right or left foot—Fig. I. The leg used in pawing is optional with the dancer. However, the same leg is used throughout each step or pawing sequence.

2. The drum beat is four steady beats with the first and third beats receiving the accent 4/4 | ♪♪♪♪ | 80. Tempo is 80 counts per minute.

3. On beat one, the dancer makes a low hop on his L foot and at the same time raises his R knee to his abdomen—Fig. II. During this movement the R foot is kept parallel with the ground, causing the knee to be sharply bent.

4. On beat two, the dancer reaches out a short distance with his R leg and lowers his R foot to the ground about 12 inches in front of his body, and then the foot is drawn or brushed backward upon the ground to its original position—Fig. III. This pawing step is done smoothly and does not resemble a stomp.

5. Repeat the above pawing step as many times as the dance requires. Remember not to alternate the leg actions.

4

Nature Dances

BUFFALO DANCE

(Plains)

Theme

No animal played a more important role in the life of the Plains Indians than did the buffalo. For these people he was the chief source of food, clothing, and shelter. The Buffalo dance was performed by the braves before going on a buffalo hunt, in appreciation and respect for this great animal. The dance also was a prayer and message to their gods reminding them that it was time for the hunt and asking them to guide the big, wandering herds close to their villages so that long distances would not have to be traveled to find them.

Two male Indians perform the dance, wearing male buffalo headdresses. The dancers' movements clearly resemble the actions of the bull buffalo as he grazes, paws the earth, and fights over possession of the herd.

Outfit

In this dance the basic outfit consists of a buffalo head, arm bands, arm cuffs, breechclout, ankle bells, fetlocks, moccasins, furpieces tied to knees, hand rattle and a bow. Marks on body are painted and may be put on with poster paint.

Procedure

1. The Buffalo dance is performed by two male dancers who line up, one behind the other, at *A*. In the starting position the dancers' bodies are

bent forward from the hips and their knees are bent so that they are in a
crouching position. The bow is held in the left hand and the rattle in the
right hand. The bow is held perpendicular to the ground with its lower
point off the ground.

2. At the start of the drum beat, the two dancers walk into the dance
area and proceed to B; the position of B is optional. They do not walk in a
straight line, but move from side to side. They remain in the crouched
position and at irregular intervals they bend their knees, lower their heads
and crouch low as would a grazing buffalo. They do not follow or mimic
each other, but walk and graze separately. While progressing from A to B,
they shake their rattles in time with the drum beat. The drum beat is
steady with a medium fast tempo, 4/4 | ♩ ♩ ♩ ♩ | 120. The dancers take
120 steps per minute or two steps each second.

3. At B, the dancers stand side by side, both facing front. They stand
erect with their heads held high and proud. Their arms are bent at the

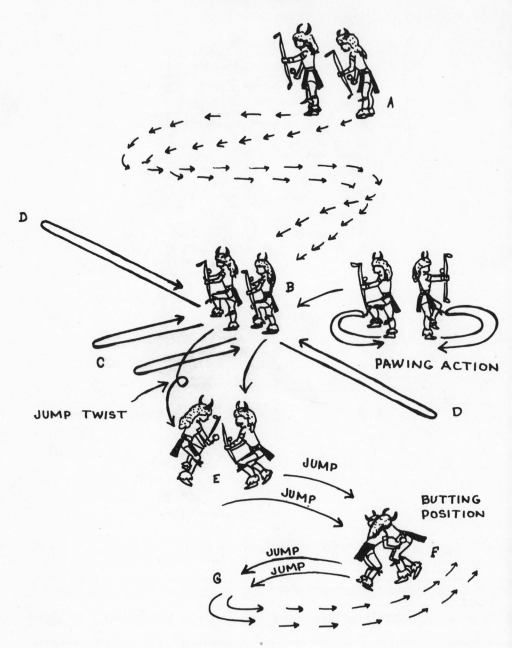

elbows, with the forearms held parallel to the ground. They hold their
bows and arrows perpendicular to the ground. Maintaining this erect position, the braves execute three Foot-and-Heel Shuffle steps (Chap. 3), drum
beat 8/8 | ♩ ♩ ♪ ♪ ♪ᵧ | 120, moving to C. Using one shuffle step, they
turn away from each other to face in the opposite direction, then using three
more shuffle steps they return to B. At this point, using another shuffle
step, they make a half-turn toward each other until they are again facing
front. The progress from B to C to B involves eight shuffle steps.

During procedure 3 the only variations to the straight and proud body position are the accented hip actions required to perform the shuffle step and the up and down movement of the right forearm that is used to shake the rattle. The arm actions shake the rattle and the leg actions shake the ankle bells and, combined, they accentuate the delightful rhythm of the dance. Throughout the remainder of the dance the bow is held as steady as possible, whereas the rattle is shaken continuously, in time with the different drum beats.

4. Each dancer now shifts his body weight to his outside foot which becomes his pivot foot, and using eight Pawing steps (Chap. 3), drum beat 4/4 | ♪ ♪ ♪ ♪ | 80, the right-hand dancer pivots counterclockwise while the dancer on the left pivots clockwise. They pivot halfway around or 180°. Without changing the pivot foot, the dancers now reverse the direction of the pivot and with eight more Pawing steps return to their original positions, facing front.

5. Each dancer stands with his body weight resting upon his inside foot and with the toe of the outside foot touching the ground, or if preferred, about eight inches off the ground. Holding this position, the dancers execute four sideward hops away from each other to D. The drummer strikes four heavy beats upon the drum as the dancers make the hops. The four hops are fast and should be completed in about one second.

6. After reaching D, the dancers, with their weight upon their outside feet, repeat the Pawing steps. The dancer on the right turns to the left or counterclockwise, and the dancer on the left turns clockwise. The dancers use eight Pawing steps and complete a full circle so that they are again facing forward.

7. The dancers, after having completed the circling, shift the weight of their bodies to the outside feet, and with four side hops return to B.

8. Repeat Pawing and circling as in procedure 4.

9. The dancers bend their knees and as the drummer strikes one heavy beat upon the drum, they jump forward three to four feet to E. The dancer on the right jumps first and is followed immediately by the dancer on the left. During the jump, they turn or twist in the air, so that upon landing they are facing each other and their feet are widely separated to give them balance.

10. While the drummer strikes four quick but heavy beats upon the drum, the two dancers lock their left shoulders together, the dancer on the left moving forward to place his left shoulder against the left shoulder of his opponent, and shove or butt each other on each drum beat. During this butting, they do not attempt to knock the other dancer out of position. The butting is performed by jumping upward and forward against each other. At each jump or butt they leave the ground about eight inches. (Refer to F for the butting positions of the dancers.)

11. The drummer strikes one loud beat and the dancer on the right jumps or springs backward about four feet to *F*. He is immediately followed by the dancer on the left. They again lock their left shoulders and repeat the four quick butting actions, accompanied by the drummer as in procedure 10.

12. The dancer on the left now jumps backward about four feet to *G*, and he is followed by the other dancer. The butting and drumming action is repeated. This third butting action completes the dance. The dancers turn, and shaking their rattles, together they walk from the dance area.

DANCE OF THE DYING EAGLE

(Plains)

Theme

To the Indian the eagle was a sacred bird. Because it could fly so high, and was so very cunning, it was considered an intermediate between their gods here on earth and those above. So highly prized were the feathers of this great winged creature that they were used in making the Indian war bonnets and in religious ceremonies. To obtain one of these birds was considered a great deed by the Indians and anyone doing so was considered a brave. After obtaining one of these very sacred birds, the Indian would do a dance in honor of this feathered monarch who contributed so much to his way of life. This particular Eagle Dance tells the story of the bird, his flight, and his death.

The dancer first enters with short running steps which depict the fast flight of the bird. The figure-eight movements represent the lazy motion of the eagle riding the air currents, and the straight forward directions, the forward flight of the bird. The quick stopping motion, and the movements of the arms (wings) symbolize the eagle coming down to land. After the eagle sees the hunter, the large sweeping motions that follow represent his futile attempts to gain altitude. The dancer's final, fluttering arm movements portray a wounded and dying bird.

Outfit

The Eagle Dancer wears a breechclout, knee (optional) and ankle fetlocks, a large rear bustle, moccasins, eagle head, eagle wings, black garments or black leotards, and bells.

Procedure

1. The Eagle Dance is performed by one male dancer who stands at *A* with his body bent forward from the hips, his knees slightly bent, and his

arms or wings extended sideward. At the start of the drum beat the dancer enters with short, fast running steps and proceeds to optional position *B*. The running step is done on the balls of the feet and each step is approximately 12 to 18 inches in length. During the run, the drum beat is steady and fast and varies from 280 to 300 beats per minute.

2. Upon reaching *B*, the dancer stops running and the drummer changes the drum beat. The dancer immediately begins the Toe-Heel step (Chap. 3) and moves around in a figure-eight pattern, drum beat 4/4 | ♪ ♪ ♪ ♪ | 160. While performing the Toe-Heel step, the dancer's body is bent forward from the hips, and the knees are slightly bent. The wings are held at

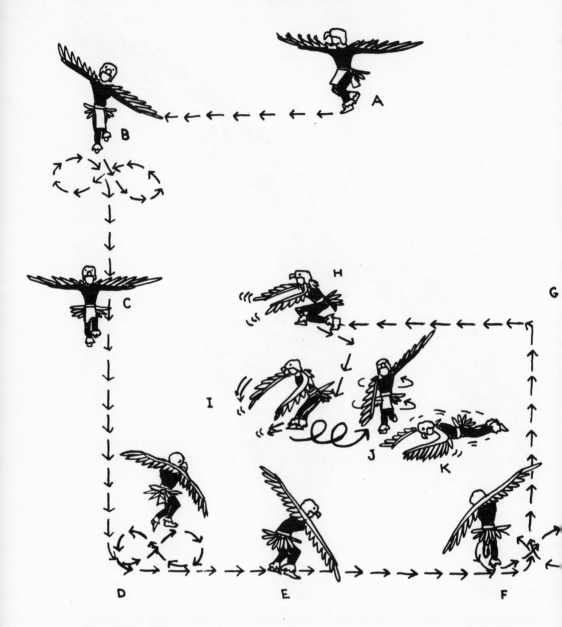

shoulder height. (Refer to *A* and notice position of wings.) As the dancer moves around the figure-eight pattern, he leans his body sideward from the hips only, toward the inside of each circle. Notice that at *B* the performer's body is leaning from the hips to the left, and left wing is dipped to the inside of the circle. As the dancer moves into the next circle of the pattern, he raises his body and wings to the upright position and then gracefully bends his body to the right or to the inside of the new circle. This is a very smooth and beautiful maneuver.

3. After completing the figure eight, the performer continues the Toe-

Heel step and moves along path C to D. While dancing along path C, the Indian bends his body from side to side. Do not drop the wings during the sideward bends but keep them at all times in a straight line with each other. Upon reaching D, and continuing the Toe-Heel step, the dancer again performs the figure-eight pattern.

4. Still using the Toe-Heel step, the dancer moves from D to E to F, repeating the actions described in procedures 2 and 3.

5. Continuing the Toe-Heel step, the dancer moves to G where he makes a 90° or quarter turn left and proceeds to H.

6. At H, the dancer stops and the drummer strikes one heavy beat upon the drum. At the heavy sound of the drum, the dancer kneels forward upon his left knee and then gracefully brings his wings to the forward position until their tips are almost touching the ground and each other. In this position, the wings are made to quiver and flutter. The fluttering is done by bending the elbows slightly and then straightening them. During the flutter, the dancer shakes or quivers his hands quickly to obtain the quivering wing action. The fluttering action is repeated eight times and along with each flutter the drummer makes a quick three beat drum roll. After each roll a slight pause is allowed, drum beat 4/4 | ♩♩♪♩♩♪ | 120. The graceful movements described above portray the frightened eagle who, after discovering the hunter below him, attempts to check his forward motion.

7. The following action is performed to four slow, but moderately heavy drum beats, and moves the dancer from H to I. At the first drum beat, the kneeling dancer stands up, stepping backward a large step with his left foot; on beat two, he steps with his right foot across in front of his left foot, placing it about two feet to the side of the left foot; on beat three, he takes a full step backward with his left foot. During this three-step action, the dancer moves to the rear and to the left a few feet from his original kneeling position with his body still facing in the same direction as before. On beat four, he again kneels to the ground on his L knee, with his wings brought forward as in procedure 6.

8. In this second kneeling position, with his wings stretched forward, the dancer slowly bends his elbows and brings the tips of his wings toward his body. He then reaches quickly sideward and around to the front, making fast, circular, sweeping actions with each of his wings. The withdrawing and circling movements of the wings against the air is performed smoothly and it is over a larger area than the fluttering and quivering actions described in procedure 6. The circling wing action is repeated eight times, and at each movement, the dancer raises his body a few inches from the ground. At the finish of the eighth circling action, the arms are brought to shoulder height and directly sideward, and the dancer should now be standing erect. The drum beat for each of the above circling actions is composed of one

soft beat followed by a heavy one, then a pause which lasts until the wings are again in the forward position. On the first soft beat the wings are pulled backward, and on the heavy beat the circling forward action takes place. During this action, the drummer should coordinate his drumming with the actions of the dancer.

9. The following action portrays the eagle being hit with an arrow; mortally wounded, he spins and falls toward the earth. With the performer standing erect, the drummer strikes one heavy beat and simultaneously the dancer drops one of his wings (optional) to his side (refer to figure at *J*); and using one foot as a pivot, he circles or spins around three times (pivot can be a hop or a buzz step). During the circling, the dancer progresses from *I* to *J*. The drummer follows the spinning action of the dancer and during each spin, strikes two fast beats upon his drum. After the third spin, the drummer strikes one loud beat on the drum, whereupon the dancer collapses and falls forward upon the ground with his wings stretched out above his head. The dancer's body and wings quiver (as at *K*) and he then lies motionless in death.

FLOWER DANCE

(Pueblo: Jemez)

Theme

Spring to the Pueblo Indians is a beautiful time of the year. The snow has melted and the warm weather has again returned to the Pueblo villages. Around these villages and upon the mountain sides the wild flowers with all the colors of the rainbow have made their appearance. In the villages appear dancers who welcome this much awaited season. They are decorated from head to foot with brightly colored wild flowers. Traditionally the white man dances around the maypole to celebrate the coming of spring. Likewise, the Pueblo Indians did a dance to honor the flowers and their god of spring.

In the Flower Dance performed by the Jemez they use five to ten dancers who are decorated with the most beautiful wild flowers which can be found. The dancers are organized in straight lines similar to the rows of flowers seen growing in the fields and along the mountain sides. During the dance the performers turn to face the east and then the west. Like growing flowers, they are following the sun which gives life to all growing things. The dancers gracefully depict flowers swaying in the breeze and their movements resemble the beauty of spring and nature herself.

Outfit

The Flower Dancers wear head and arm bands decorated with flowers. The wrist bands or cuffs have flowers painted upon them. The outfit also includes silver or turquoise necklaces, tunic, sash, boots or moccasins, and a turkey feather roach. The dancers always carry two rattles, one in each hand. This is the authentic outfit, but it is permissible to wear any standard Indian outfit to which flower decorations have been added. The dancers must have rattles and be wearing the turkey feather roach.

Procedure

1. This dance is ordinarily performed by five to ten dancers. They stand in a straight line at the south end of the dance area—*A*.

NORTH

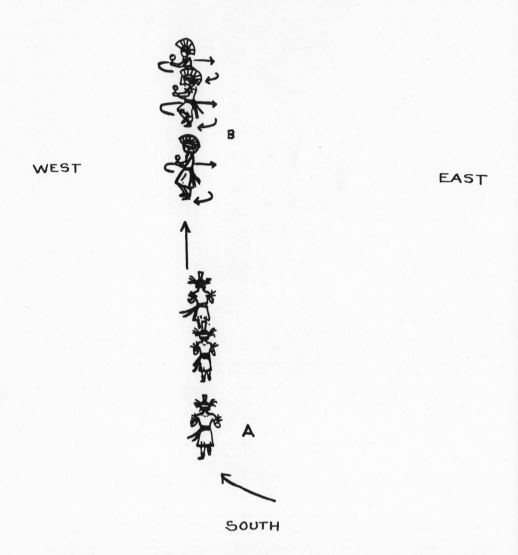

WEST

EAST

SOUTH

2. When the drum beat commences the line moves forward to *B*. They stand erect with their elbows bent and the rattles held in front of their bodies at about hip level. They use the One-Foot Stomp (Chap. 3) and shake their rattles in time with the drum and their foot movements, drum beat 4/4 | ♪ ♩ ♪ ♩ | 160 to 180 depending upon skill of dancers. While entering the dance area they bend or sway their bodies from side to side. They also turn and lean their heads in the direction of the swaying body. As the body sways to one side, the hand and rattle on that same side is lowered slightly while the other hand is raised. The direction of the sway-

ing bodies is optional. They do not all sway to the right or left at the same time.

3. At *B*, the forward progress of the line ceases. The dancers perform four One-Foot Stomp steps as they pivot left, to face west. The dancers stand in place and do eight One-Foot Stomp steps; in doing this step, they raise the left foot completely off the ground and then replace it; they do not move forward.

4. The dancers now perform eight stationary One-Foot Stomp steps without raising the left foot completely from the floor; they merely raise the left heel off the floor, and then replace it. In the remainder of the instructions the stationary One-Foot Stomp step, in which the left foot remains in contact with the ground, will be referred to as the Heel Stomp.

5. They repeat four One-Foot Stomp steps while pivoting right, to face north. In this position the dancers repeat eight One-Foot Stomp steps in place, and eight Heel Stomps in place.

6. The dancers repeat four One-Foot Stomp steps, turning to face east, and repeat the eight One-Foot Stomp steps and eight Heel-Stomps in place.

7. They repeat four One-Foot Stomp steps, again turning to face north; and then eight One-Foot Stomp steps and eight Heel-Stomps in place.

8. Then four One-Foot Stomp steps, again turning to face west.

9. Two more times they repeat procedures 3, 4, 5, 6, 7 and 8, turning from west to north to east to north to west again.

10. After having completed the third movement sequence of following the sun, the dancers use four One-Foot Stomp steps turning or pivoting left until they are facing south. In this position the line of dancers continue the One-Foot Stomp and move from the dance area. They return to *A*, their starting position.

HORSETAIL DANCE

(*Taos*)

Theme

Before the white man came the Indians did not have horses, and their only means of transportation was by walking. Then, from the South came the Spaniards, and with them came the horses. The Taos were some of the first Indians to come in contact with the exploring Spanish. They were amazed by the horse and pleased with his ability to transport. The Taos traded with the Spaniards for some of the horses. Other horses wandered off or were lost, and became the flourishing bands of wild horses to roam the

North American continent. Many of these wild horses were caught and
domesticated by the Indians, which brought about a significant change in
their lives. So grateful were the Indians for the horses that they did a
dance to honor these gallant animals.

The Taos Horsetail Dance usually is performed by several male dancers
who portray horses galloping, trotting, and bucking. Each dancer wears a
horse's tail which he swishes back and forth and up and down during the
dance. The body and foot actions along with the tail movements are imi-
tations of the actions of a real horse. Especially is this mimetic action noticeable when the dancers are portraying a backing horse. They accentuate
their hip actions to give the tail life-like movements.

Outfit

The outfit worn by the Horsetail dancer is composed of a hair roach
which represents a horse's mane, and a hair tail fastened to the lower back
of the dancer which represents a horse's tail. These and a rattle and leg

bells are necessary parts of the costume. Other suggested parts are optional, and any basic war dance outfit is acceptable. Suggested parts are a head band, arm bands, bolero, arm cuffs, breechclout, fetlocks, and moccasins.

Procedure

1. The dancers line up in a straight line, one behind the other, at *A*. At the start of the drum beat, the dancers begin the Four-Beat Stomp (Chap. 3) drum beat 4/4 | ♩ ♩ ♩ ♪ | 180, and proceed forward to *B* (optional). If dancers cannot do this step to 180 counts, slow drum beat to from 140 to 160 counts. The dancers keep in a straight line and in step with the leader. At *B* the leader executes a quarter turn left and continues dancing forward until all of the other dancers, following behind him, have completed the turn at *B* and again are in a straight line formation, facing South.

2. At *C* the leader stops and executes in place a quarter turn right. The other dancers successively make the quarter turn right until all are facing left and in a straight line.

3. The dancers, placing their hands upon their hips, with their thumbs to the rear, and bending their bodies forward from the hips, move backward to *D*, using 16 to 24 backward Toe-Heel-Chug steps (the number of backward chug steps is dependent upon the size of the dance area).

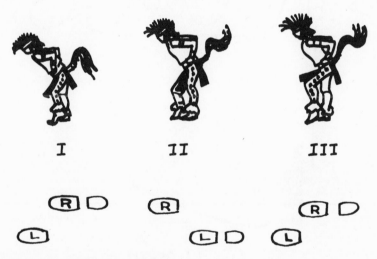

I   II   III

Backward Toe-Heel-Chug Step

a. Starting position—Fig. I. The dancer stands with both feet together, with the weight upon the R foot. The L knee is bent with the ball of the L foot resting lightly upon the ground. The L hip is lowered and the R hip is raised. The hands are placed upon the hips with the thumbs facing forward. The body leans forward from the hips.

b. The drum beat is four steady, medium loud beats, 4/4 | ♩ ♩ ♩ ♩ | 160.

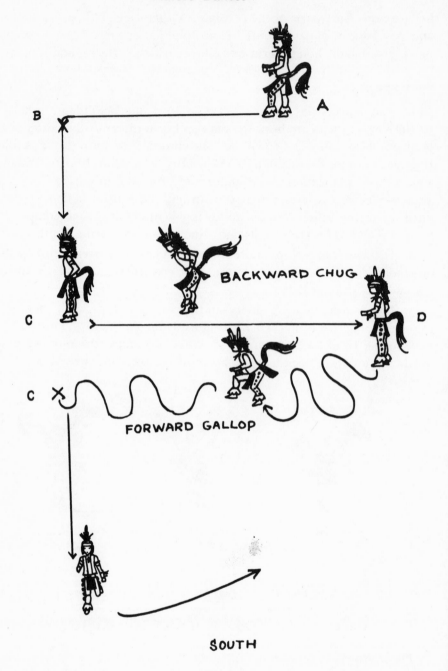

SOUTH

c. On beat one, the L foot is drawn or shuffled backward about 8 inches—Fig. II. During the shuffle the body weight is shifted from the R to the L foot. The L knee is straightened and the R knee is bent. During this movement the R hip is lowered while the L hip is sharply raised. The action of bringing the L leg backward and the exaggerated movement of raising the hips places the L hip farther to the rear than the

R hip. The dancer actually leads with the hip as he does the backward shuffle and this movement causes the tail to bounce up and down and to swish back and forth.

    d. On beat two, shuffle the R foot backward, repeating the above procedure—Fig. III.

    e. On beats three and four, repeat the above procedures.

4. At *D* the dancers stop and stand erect. At the start of the drum beat they do 8 to 12 forward gallop steps back to *C* (the number of gallop steps taken is one-half the number of backward chug steps). The gallop is performed with high knee lifts, long or big steps and with the knees turned outward. The big steps carry the dancers from side to side. Arm action is up and down and it is done forcefully as also is the leg action.

5. Procedures 3 and 4 are repeated two more times.

6. At the completion of the three movements of backing up and galloping forward, the dancers turn left, and dance from the area, keeping a straight line and using the Four-Beat Stomp (refer to procedure 1).

HUNTING DANCE

(*Pawnee*)

Theme

Most of the large animals of America played an important part in the lives of the American Indians. They were their chief source of food and clothing. One of the animals of greatest importance to the Pawnee Indians was the deer. His hide provided the buckskin outfits that kept the Pawnee warm during the cold months, and he provided the meat that carried him through the long winter.

Before going on a deer hunt, the Pawnee Indians did a dance in which they depicted a successful and happy hunt. This dance was also performed as a tribute to this fine animal; as a demonstration of the skill of their hunters; and as a prayer of thanks to their gods.

The dance represents a deer hunt in which both the hunted and hunter perform. It shows the graceful movements of the deer, his pawing of the earth, his slow grazing, and upon suddenly becoming frightened, his quick bounding retreat to avoid the hunters. The hunters also are portrayed tracking the deer, pointing their bows and arrows, making wind checks, and going through the activities of a successful hunt.

Outfits

The deer dancers wear a deer headdress, arm bands, cuffs, breechclout, knee and ankle fur pieces, ankle bells, belt, and moccasins, and have designs painted on the body. Deer hunters can wear and standard outfit but must carry a bow and arrow. The hunters wear a headband with two feathers, arm bands, breechclout, bolero, leggings, belt, and moccasins, and carry a bow and arrow.

Procedure

1. This dance is performed by approximately four Indians portraying the deer and six to' twelve Indians as hunters (optional). The two separate groups perform different patterns. Check the pattern illustrating this dance and notice that *A*, *B* and *C* indicate the pattern for the deer dancers, and the small *a*, *b* and *c* the pattern followed by the hunters. At *A*, the deer line up with one lead dancer standing in front and the others stand-

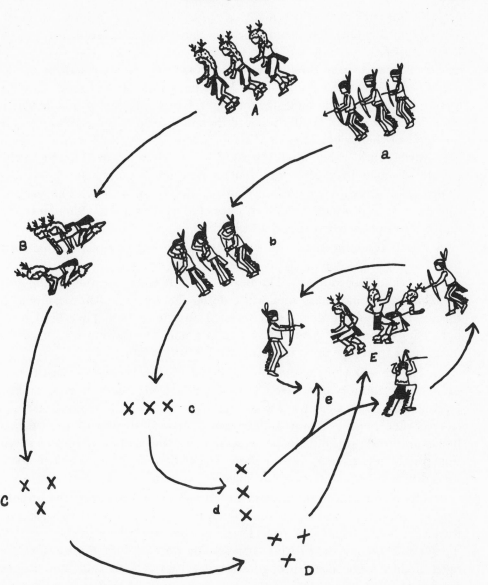

ing in a straight line behind him. At *a*, the hunters stand close together
as an informal group without any particular formation. The hunters retain this informal grouping throughout the dance except when they form
a circle upon reaching position *e*.

2. At the beginning of the dance, the deer enter using the One-Foot
Stomp (Chap. 3) drum beat 4/4 | ♪ ♩ ♪ ♩ | 160, and proceed forward from
point *A* to *B*. Throughout procedures 2 to 8 and without a change or
break, the drummer maintains this steady rhythm. Distances moved
throughout this dance are optional and depend upon the size of the dance
area. After the deer move into the dance area they do not remain in a

straight line but move informally with the lead deer always in front. Throughout the One-Foot Stomp the deer dancers usually stand straight but it is permissible for each dancer to vary his body position as he desires. He may lean forward from the hips and also exaggerate his knee actions and in this way increase the up and down bobbing action of the body. For example, if the stomp is made by the right foot being raised and lowered, some dancers will lean farther forward than others, and some will exaggerate the bend of their right knee as the foot is raised; and they will also bend both knees considerably when the right foot is stomped or lowered to the ground. Immediately after the foot strikes the ground, the knees are straightened, thus giving the body an up and down action. The dancers who use this step should remain in a low crouch throughout the dance except at position E when they stand erect.

3. Upon reaching B, the deer stop their forward progress and perform four Pawing steps (Chap. 3) in time with the drum beat, which remains the same as in procedure 2. The beat is soft. It is permissible for the deer to pivot on the stationary foot while doing the pawing. After completing the pawing steps, the deer kneel forward on one or both knees and place both hands upon the ground. In this position they lower their heads to the ground and move them from side to side as if grazing.

4. The kneeling of the deer is the signal for the hunters to begin their dance. The hunters move from a to b while using the One-Foot Stomp. During the step they crouch low and hold their bows and arrows directly in front of their bodies. As the hunters dance forward, they turn or twist their bodies from side to side and point their bows and arrows in various directions as though aiming. Throughout the dance, hunters and deer adapt their different body and foot movements to the same drum beat.

5. Upon reaching b, about eight to ten feet behind the deer, the hunters stop to check the wind direction. They toss imaginary sand or dust into the air, or hold a handful at arm's length and let it sift through their fingers. They shade their eyes with one hand while peering into the distance for signs of deer. The deer throughout this action remain calm and in the grazing position.

6. After testing the wind, the hunters, using the One-Foot Stomp, move toward the deer. The deer hear the hunters coming and they become frightened. The deer turn their heads toward the hunters, quickly stand up and sniff the air. They nervously look around and suddenly, using the One-Foot Stomp, they dance away from the hunters and proceed to C. When fleeing, the deer double the number of stomp steps usually danced to the set tempo, thus moving faster than the hunters. It is also permissible to retain the same step and tempo as the hunters, but increase the length of the step.

7. The deer repeat the action of fleeing, pawing and grazing two more times as the hunters follow them and repeat their actions of tracking, pointing, and seeking.

8. At *E*, while the deer are grazing for the fourth time, the hunters catch up to them. The hunters separate, some of them circling to the right and the others to the left until they have completely encircled the deer.

9. The frightened deer stand up and begin running, jumping, and attempting to escape. The hunters, performing a fast Toe-Heel step (Chap. 3) move counterclockwise around the deer, drum beat 4/4 | ♩♪♩♪ | 240. The count for this step is usually 160 counts per minute, but for this dance it should be 240 as indicated. If dancers cannot do the step at 240 counts, cut the tempo as needed. While moving around the circle, the hunters keep pointing their arrows at the deer. Since the deer are moving in several different directions, the bow actions change from side to side as the hunters aim at the deer. The drummer continues the drum beat until the hunters have circled the deer three times. He then strikes one heavy beat upon the drum. At the sound of the heavy drum beat, the hunters utter a shrill cry, and at the same time lunge forward on their left feet toward the encircled deer. They forcefully straighten their arms toward one of the fleeing deer but do not release the arrow. This action portrays the shooting of the deer. The deer immediately fall to the ground dead.

10. Without drum beats, the hunters happily move forward and, pairing up, they drag or carry the dead deer from the area.

MOUNTAIN SHEEP DANCE

(Piute)

Theme

In the area of the Piute Indians roamed the mountain sheep. They were an important source of food for these Indians of the Great Basin west of the Wasatch Mountains. Many miles were sometimes traveled by the tribes to the cliffs and ledges where these fleet-footed animals lived. The Piute Indians did a dance to represent this hunt, and it is one of the most primitive of the Indian dances.

In the dance pattern below, the hunters are pictured as they hold out their bows in anticipation of finding the mountain sheep. A ram comes bounding onto the scene and is followed by the hunters with their bows. The dance portrays the shooting at the ram as he comes into view of the

hunters, followed by the checking of the arrows for signs of blood. One of the unusual aspects of the dance is that the bloody arrow is found before the ram is ever killed. Logically, a bloody arrow would indicate that the sheep had been killed, thus completing a successful hunt. Why the bloody arrow is found before the ram is killed is something not understood, but this is the Indians' way and is one of the primitive aspects of the dance.

Outfits

For this dance, the mountain sheep, or ram, wears a horned headdress, belt, a long breechclout, a half or short tunic, and moccasins, and has designs painted on the body. The hunters wear a headband with two feathers, breechclout, wrist band, moccasins, have painted body designs, and carry a bow and arrow and a quiver with additional arrows.

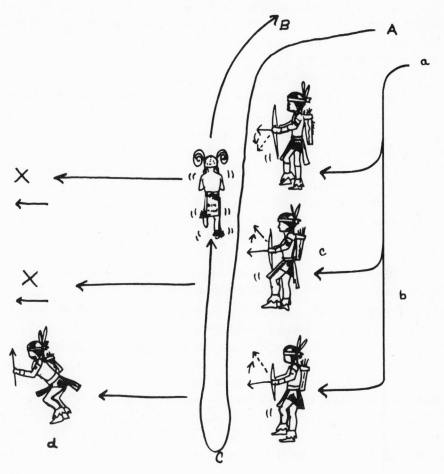

Procedure

1. The mountain Sheep Dance is performed by one dancer who represents the mountain sheep (ram) and usually five hunters. More hunters may be used if desired. The ram and hunters line up at positions *A* and *a*, respectively.

2. To start the dance the hunters, without drum accompaniment, and holding their bows in shooting position, walk into the dance area from *a* to *b*. At *b*, they stop and stand in a straight line facing front; then, starting with the head dancer, one after another they execute a quarter turn right and move to *c*. They keep the bow and arrow in shooting position with the bow slightly drawn.

3. At this point the mountain sheep dancer, using the Four-Beat Stomp (Chap. 3) drum beat 4/4 | ♩ ♩ ♩ ♪ | 100, moves out from *A* and dances forward to *B*, on to *C* where he makes a right turn, and dances back to *B*. During this entire movement from *B* to *C* to *B*, the hunters stand with their bows and arrows pointing at the moving ram.

4. After the sheep has returned to B, the drum beat stops and the hunters, one at a time, starting with the lead brave, walk forward three steps to d and place their arrows upon the ground as shown in the dance pattern. After each brave places his arrow he steps three steps backward to his original position in the line.

5. The lead hunter leaves the front of the line and walks around the front of the row of arrows and proceeds to the last arrow. Picking the arrows up one by one, from back to front, he carefully examines each for signs of blood. He holds each arrow before his face and slowly examines it. Finding no signs of blood, he shakes his head negatively and returns the arrow to its original position upon the ground. He examines his own arrow last and, after setting it down, he steps three steps backward to his front position in the line. Moving as a unit the hunters step forward three steps and together they pick up their arrows. They now take three steps backward to their original position. Upon their return, they place the arrow to the bow string and raise the bow again to the shooting position. As the hunters raise their bows, the drum beat recommences.

6. The ram repeats the dancing from B to C to B, and the hunters follow with procedures 4 and 5, two more times.

7. The third time that the lead brave walks out and examines the arrows for blood, he discovers it. He usually finds it upon the second arrow he examines. Upon finding the bloodstained arrow, he holds it in his right hand, and waving it above his head, he utters a piercing scream ("Aah-weee-yah"). The hunters immediately rush forward and pick up their arrows and return to their positions in the line. The braves, keeping their steps together, perform in place a fast One-Foot Stomp (Chap. 3) drum beat 4/4 | ♪♩♪♩ | 180.

8. At the start of the fast drum beat, the ram, using the Toe-Heel step (Chap. 3) dances forward until he is directly in front of the line of hunters. At this point he begins dancing around, remaining in a small area. As the ram dances in front of them, the hunters, using the One-Foot Stomp, quickly encircle the ram.

9. While circling the ram, the braves make shooting movements with their bows and arrows. Finally, the ram falls and the hunters run forward, and taking him by his legs and arms, carry him from the dance area. The drummer strikes a loud beat as the ram falls and then the drum is silent.

SNAKE DANCE

(*Nambee*)

Theme

To the Indians, the snake was more than just a reptile. They believed that he lived so close to the ground he understood the problems of the soil and its need for water before it could grow plants. The Indian did the snake dance to influence the snake to carry a message to the gods in their behalf, that the soil was dry and parched and needed rain.

The dancers, while performing the snake dance, use motions imitative of a crawling snake. They portray the snake coiling, striking, retreating and returning to strike again.

Outfit

The outfit for this dance is composed of a chief's bonnet, skirt, sash, knee fur pieces, ankle bells, fetlocks, moccasins, and arm bands and beads, or any standard war dance outfit plus a chief's bonnet, and a rattle and a 16-inch wooden stick with two colored feathers attached.

Procedure

1. The dance is performed by three male dancers who line up one behind the other at *A*. At the start of the drum beat, the dancers, using the War Dance step, the Variation step, the Canoe step, the Cross-Over Sti-yu, or the Four-Beat Stomp (Chap. 3) drum beat 4/4 | ♩ ♩ ♩ ♪ | 120, enter and move across the dance area. At an optional point, depending upon the size of the area, the line turns or circles left and moves to the center of the area, *B*.

2. At *B*, the performers stop their forward motion, and keeping with the drum beat, make a clockwise turn until facing front.

3. Without stopping the drum beat or the War Dance step, the three dancers form a triangle. The second Indian dances in place, while the first and third separate and move seven steps to *C* and *D*, and on the eighth step they turn around and face the center of the triangle, *E*.

4. The three dancers, using fifteen War Dance steps (Chap. 3) and weaving a snake-like path, move to the center of the triangle. As they weave like a crawling snake, each dancer bends sideward, and leans his arms and body to the inside of each curve or turn. Throughout the dance, the drummer and the dancers do not change the drum beat nor the dance step. However, at this center position, the drummer strikes one loud beat, and the dancers strike or lunge at each other. The strike is performed by each

dancer making one quick step toward the center of the triangle with the head thrust forward and low, like that of a striking snake.

5. The dancers, performing eight War Dance steps, reverse direction, and in a direct line proceed to their original positions around the triangle.

6. They repeat procedures 3 and 4, three times.

7. Upon completion of the fourth time through, the dancers re-form their line at *B*. The second brave dances in place while the other two dancers return to their original positions in front of and behind him. This action should be completed with 16 War Dance steps.

8. To complete the dance, the first dancer leads the other two from the area with the War Dance step along a serpentine path, *F*.

5

Religious Dances

CHIEF DANCE

(Sioux)

Theme

Most cultures and societies have some form of leadership, and so it was with the Indians. This leadership was embodied in the tribal chief who was elevated to his position as a result of some great deed, prophecy, vision, or by vote of the people. The Chief Dance demonstrates that authority.

During the dance the chief appears in all the splendor of his native dress, war bonnet, eagle wand, beaded finery, and a beautifully fringed buckskin outfit. With dignity, he parades before the spectators. He dances a slow, stately Toe-and-Heel Shuffle step, during which he gracefully raises his head, arms and wand up and down, and then from side to side. Also, he makes large sweeping motions with his eagle wand. These stately and proud movements represent authority; they symbolize the high esteem that accompanies being chief. Following the slow, stately step, the chief moves into a fast War Dance. This is a demonstration to the young warriors that he can still compete with them, and that authority is not to be disputed.

Outfit

The chief wears a chief's war bonnet, war shirt, leggings, breechclout, belt, neck beads, and moccasins, and carries in his right hand an eagle-feathered wand.

Procedure

1. The dance can be performed by a chief or several chiefs. When several chiefs perform this dance, they work together and follow the same pattern. They keep in a line, and all move together in the same direction and keep in step with the lead chief. They line up at *A* with the leader in the rear. They walk forward to *B*, where the line turns left, and proceed to *C*, where the line halts. Together they make another quarter turn left. If only one chief is dancing, he walks to *B*, makes the turn, and walks to *C*, where he makes the quarter turn left. The following procedures are for a single chief dancer.

2. The chief, standing tall and stately at *A*, begins his chief walk. He enters the area, and maintaining his stately posture, walks to points *B* and

then C. At C he turns left, facing the right side of the area. This part of the dance is done without drum accompaniment.

3. As the chief turns and faces the right side of the area the drummer starts a soft but steady drum beat. The chief immediately progresses forward across the area, using a very slow Heel-Shuffle step (Chap. 3) drum beat 4/4 | ♩ ♩̂ ♩ ♩̂ | 80. Upon reaching D, the chief makes a right turn, and then dances back to C. During this entire movement and in time with his foot actions, the chief bends his body forward and downward and back upward. While doing the bends and keeping in time with his steps, he sways his body from side to side. The arm and hand actions follow the body and foot actions. For example, as the body leans forward, the hands

are extended forward. They are directed also toward the foot actions. As the right foot is placed forward the arms and hands are lowered and pointed in that direction. As the two arms are lowered to the right or left sides, they are held at similar height. When the chief raises his body upward, the left hand is raised about shoulder height, but the right hand with the wand is raised above the head and to the left side. While it is held in this position, the chief eyes the wand proudly. The above bending, straightening, and other movements are repeated several times as the dancer moves from C to D to C.

4. The dancer repeats procedure 3.

5. The chief again turns at C and proceeds to D. This is the third time the chief has been at D position. As he reaches this point, the drummer starts a loud and fast drum beat. The chief turns and using a fast, War Dance step or the Variation (Chap. 3), or the Cross-Over Sti-yu, moves from D to C to D to C. Drum beat 4/4 | ♩ ♩ ♩ ♪ | 200.

6. As the chief reaches C, the drummer resumes the beat for the slow, Heel-Toe Shuffle step, and using this step, the chief makes a half turn left and dances from the area. He continues the bending movement as described in procedure 3.

MESCALERO GAN DANCE
or
MOUNTAIN SPIRITS

(Apache Devil Dance)

Theme

The Apache Indians believed strongly in devils and mountain spirits, and so they danced to ward off these evil spirits. The Devil Dance also was performed as part of the purity rites for young girls of the tribe. At the age of 16, young maidens of the tribe were honored into womanhood and protected from evil spirits by the Devil Dancers.

During this dance the male dancers move away from the maidens and can be seen making menacing gestures and taunting movements to drive away evil spirits. Later in the dance the men again join with the girls, and the jumping and poking actions they direct at the maidens are only teasing and tempting gestures. During this action it is interesting to watch the maidens ignore and act unconcerned about the taunting gestures of the devils.

Outfit

The Devil or Gan outfit is composed of a devil headpiece, wooden hand wands, red cloth streamers with feathers, belt with bells, tunic with bells, sash, boot-type moccasins and knee bells under the tunic; and the dancer has designs painted on the body.

The maidens may wear a yellow or white dress trimmed with fringe, and moccasins. Indian maidens usually wear a white or yellow buckskin outfit profusely decorated with bead work.

Procedure

1. At *A* the dancers line up in single file with each maiden followed by her male (devil) dancer. At the start of the drum beat, which is a long heavy drum roll, the girls, followed by the men, proceed to *B*; the girls, standing erect and stately, walk to *B*, the male dancers use exaggerated sideward hopping steps. They step diagonally to the right with the right foot

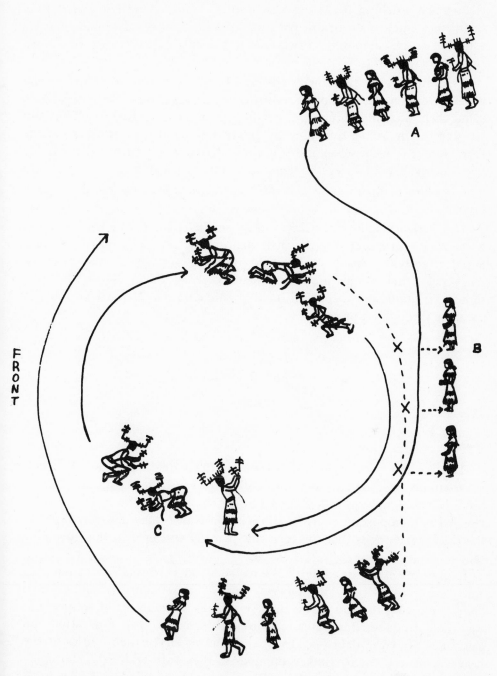

and hop on it, then they step diagonally to the left with the left foot and hop on it. While doing this sideward hop-step they raise their knees high, almost as though galloping. They also lower their arms and raise them high over their heads causing the body to fold and straighten during the hop-step. After the group has reached *B*, the drum roll is changed to a steady beat of approximately 160 beats per minute, 4/4 | ♩ ♩ ♩ ♩ | 160.

2. Upon reaching *B* the maidens step sideward to the left about three small steps and remain in this position without moving. The male dancers continue several hop-steps forward, and keeping in single file they turn right and circle to *C*.

3. From *C* the male dancers continue to move around the circle, completing three circles (optional). During the circling they dance separately using their own individual and original devil-like movements. They use all types of menacing and taunting body and hand actions. They shake their wands, crouch, stoop and squat low, bend from side to side, and use hops and exaggerated steps, to depict the actions of devils.

4. At the completion of the circling the maidens walk forward and their male partners fall in behind them as in their original position at *A*.

5. The dancers move in a large clockwise circle, and then leave the dance area. As the group circles, the male dancers use the exaggerated sideward hop-step and also make teasing and taunting gestures at the maidens. They poke their wands and jump menacingly at them. The girls walk, showing disdain and unconcern for the male dancers. Drum beat remains the same throughout procedures 2 to 5.

RAIN DANCE

(*Zuni*)

Theme

The Indians of the arid Southwest were dependent upon corn for their main supply of food. In the spring they planted their corn in hills or small bunches and depended upon rain to come and make it grow. They realized how important rain was to their survival so they danced to inform the Kachinas or gods that the corn was planted and needed the life-giving rain.

In the dance, the priest leads the dancers and performs acts of planting and sowing the seed. The dancers' turning movements symbolize corn plants following the sun across the sky. Their scooping hand actions portray the corn's need for water to drink. One of the most interesting and colorful acts of the dance occurs as the dancers shake their rattles at the heavens and cry out to awaken the gods so they will send down the much needed rain.

Outfits

The rain dancers wear a Kachina mask, tunic, sash, moccasins, knee and leg bells, and painted arm bands, and have designs painted upon their chest, shoulders, and back. They carry a rattle in the left hand.

The priest wears the same outfit as the other dancers except he doesn't wear a mask or carry a rattle. He carries a medium sized basket containing corn meal.

Procedure

1. The group stands in a straight line at *A,* facing north. The priest is the leader. At the start of the drum beat, the priest walks into the area, followed by the five rain dancers (the number of rain dancers is optional). As the priest walks, he carries the basket cradled in his left arm and hand. He continually puts his R hand into the basket, and withdrawing it, he makes movements as though sprinkling corn upon the ground before him and in the path of the dancers. The rain dancers follow the priest. They do not walk but perform the One-Foot Stomp (Chap. 3) drum beat 4/4 | ♪ ♪ ♪ ♩ | 160, while constantly shaking their rattles.

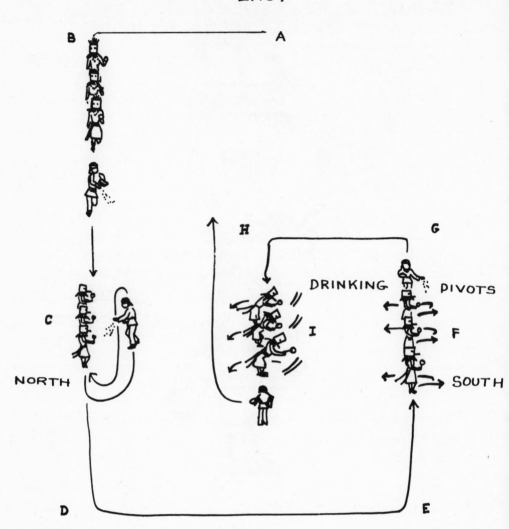

EAST

WEST

2. Upon reaching *B*, the line turns left and proceeds to *C*. At this point the line stops its forward motion, but the rain dancers continue in place with four stomp steps, while making a quarter turn left, to face south.

3. The dancers continue the stomp step in place as the priest makes a left turn and walks up and back in front of them. As he walks he keeps turning and glancing at the line of dancers and spreading corn meal before them. This action symbolizes fertility of the seed. Upon reaching the other end of the line, the priest turns left and sows corn while returning to the head of the line. Dancers now place rattles in their **R** hands.

4. The priest again stands at the head of the line. The dancers, using four stomp steps, make a quarter turn right, to face west.

5. The priest, walking and spreading corn, leads the dancers from *C* to *D*, *E*, and *F*. At *F*, the line stops its forward progress. The priest, as in procedure 3, sows corn back and forth in front of the braves, or along the south side of the group. As the priest sows corn, the dancers, using four stomp steps, first pivot to the left and face north; then using eight more stomp steps, they turn right and face front, or south. The dancers, again using four stomp steps, turn left facing the east. The priest, during the above action, continues sowing corn in front of them until he again reaches the east end of the line; he then returns to resume his leadership at the head of the line. The dancers do not at any time stop the dance step; they do not rest between turns.

6. The priest, sowing corn, leads the line of dancers from *F* to *G*, *H*, and *I*. The priest turns around and faces the line of dancers. During the following procedures the priest stands and watches the action. He does not sow corn.

7. The dancers use four stomp steps while making a left turn in place, to face south; the priest is facing east. The drummer stops the beat and the performers stop dancing the stomp step.

8. Keeping together, the dancers now step forward with their left feet. They bend the left knee sharply, lean forward and stoop low, their left hands extended forward and their right hands extended to the rear. With the right hand vigorously shaking the rattle, it is brought forward close to the ground in a scooping action. They continue the movement until the rattle is brought up to the lips, with the head held high, as in a drinking position. This action symbolizes that the plants need to drink water. With the rattle held in the drinking position, the dancers, still keeping together, slowly rise to standing, bringing the left foot back beside the right. The drum is started again and the dancers, using eight stomp steps, pivot right in place, to face north.

9. Facing north, they repeat the scooping as in procedure 8 (no drum).

10. The drum beat resumes and the dancers, using eight stomp steps, pivot left in place, to face south.

11. The drummer strikes one heavy beat as the dancers altogether step forward with their left foot and at the same time bring their right hand forcefully forward and up. During this action, they shake the rattles and utter a loud scream ("O weeee yaaa"). The cry is made to awaken the Kachinas or gods who live in the clouds, so they will send rain to the earth.

12. The dancers step back in place, turn right and face west; the priest turns and takes his place at the head of the line. The drumming starts and the dancers, using the stomp step, follow the priest from the area. The priest sows corn before the dancers as he leads them away.

6

Social and Comic Dances

BELT DANCE

(Pueblo: Tewa)

Theme

The Pueblo Indians were famous for their weaving and embroidery. They developed the art long before the white man came to America. Other Indian tribes traded with the Pueblos to obtain their woven goods. The Pueblos wove long belts about four inches wide and six to eight feet long. These long belts, which actually resemble narrow sashes, were beautifully made from brightly colored yarns. Many tribes traded for these belts and used them when dancing the Belt Dance.

The Pueblo-Tewa Belt Dance is a social dance performed by three male and three female dancers. During the dance the long belts are held at one end by the women while their men partners wind and unwind them while smoothly performing a Toe-Heel dance step. As the dance progresses the men performers with the help of the women also braid and unbraid the belts. The beautiful steps and formations, and the winding and braiding of the belts, represent the tribe's skill and knowledge of weaving. The dancers take great pride in their ability to perform this dance without making an error.

Outfits

The male dance outfit may be any standard male outfit plus a long belt or a long cloth sash and a hair roach. The outfit shown includes a belt, hair roach, arm bands, cuffs, bolero, breechclout, leg bells, fetlocks, ankle bells, and moccasins.

The female outfit may be any standard female buckskin dress or any simple tan or white cloth dress.

88

Procedure

1. The six dancers line up in a straight line at *A*. The man stands in front of his woman partner. With both hands the men hold the folded belt directly in front of their bodies at about waist height.

2. The musician starts the drum beat 4/4 | ♪ ♪ ♪ ♪ | 160, and continues this throughout the dance. Once the performers have started the dance they continue their steps until they have left the dance area. During the entire dance the men use the Toe-Heel step (Chap. 3) and the women do a low, short running step. Using these two steps the dancers proceed to B where they stop their forward dance motion and make a one quarter turn right. During the progress from *A* to *B* the men sway from side to side. While they do the Toe-Heel step they move or swing their body, hands, arms, and belt toward the forward foot. For example, as the left

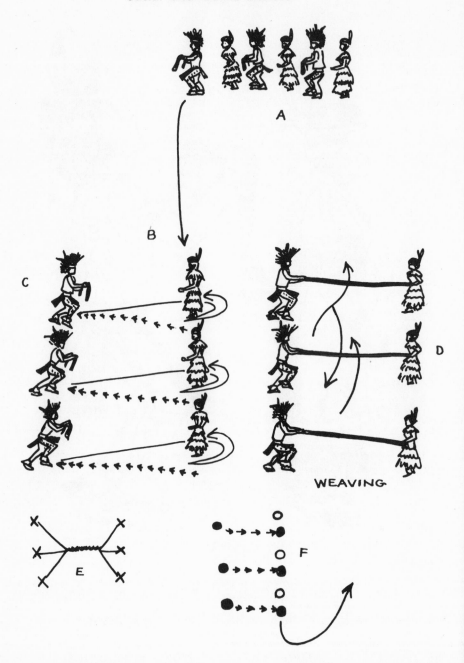

foot is placed forward, the two hands also are extended in that direction and the body and face are turned and bent to the left. As the right foot is placed forward, the hands and body actions are to the right. If inexperienced dancers cannot do the Toe-Heel step to the fast 160 tempo, cut it to 140 counts per minute.

3. The women use a stationery low running step at *B* while the men dance forward, using eight Toe-Heel steps, to *C* where they turn right to

face the women. Remember that the men and women continue their dance steps without stopping during the entire dance.

4. The men do four steps in place and then dance forward to their women partners; upon reaching their partners, they each place the end of their belt, held by their L hand, into the L hand of their partner.

5. Each man, holding the other end of his belt with his R hand and with his L hand holding the belt about two feet above the R hand, dances clockwise around his woman partner, wrapping the belt around her waist. When the belt is wrapped completely around her waist he reverses his direction and unwinds it.

6. The men take the belts from the women, and turning away from them, again dance to C.

7. They repeat procedures 4 and 5.

8. The second time the men unwind the belt from around their partners, the women do not release their end of the belt but hold on to it. The men, as in procedure 6, turn and dance toward C, but they only progress as far as the belt will allow them. They now make a right turn and face their women partners, as shown at D.

9. At D, the two end male dancers face the center man, and continuing the dance step, they braid the belts as shown in the diagram E. The first dancer starts the braid by holding his belt high and dancing forward and over the second (center) man who has faced him. The second man dances to the first one's position and turns right, to face the action. At the time the first man reaches the center position he drops low while the third man moves above and past him. This now puts the third man in the center, the first man in the third man's old position and the second in the first one's original position. The three male dancers continue the weaving of the belt with the outside men always weaving over and the inside person going under.

10. After the braid is completed the dancers reverse their actions and unbraid the belts.

11. The dancers are again arranged as shown at D. The men dance in place as the women spin clockwise, allowing the belts to wrap around their waists, until they reach the male dancers. At this point the women immediately reverse their spin and unwind the belts, returning to their original positions.

12. The men now dance forward and with their L hand grasp the belt about two feet from the end the women are holding. The women release the belt and the men hold it in a folded position in front of their bodies. The men now move in front of their partners, as in the diagram F, and continuing the dance steps, the group leaves the area.

LOST TOMAHAWK

(Plains)

Theme

The tomahawk was one of the Indians' most valued implements. It served him in war, and in hunting and working. A brave seldom went anywhere without his tomahawk. It became so dear to him that he took great pride in caring for and protecting it. He kept it sharp, clean, and beautifully decorated. The Lost Tomahawk is a dance performed in respect for this useful tool. The dancer exhibits deep pride and admiration for his cherished tomahawk. It is interesting to see the emotion he displays when he discovers another Indian admiring it. He shows great anxiety and bravery, then disdain toward the other Indian. Upon losing his tomahawk he exhibits wild and excited movements until he has found it. The scalping scene portrays to what extent a brave will go to regain his beloved tomahawk.

Outfit

The outfit for this dance is any standard war dance outfit without bustle. The lead dancer must have a tomahawk and be wearing leg or knee and ankle bells. Besides these required articles, the lead dancer usually wears a hair roach, breechclout, yoke, fetlocks, armbands, cuffs, and moccasins.

Procedure

1. This dance has a lead dancer, three watchers, an accomplice and, if available, an audience. The audience may be composed of other Indian performers, or if practical, spectators. The four active performers line up at *A*, with the three watchers standing in a row at the right of the lead dancer. The audience sits cross-legged upon the ground to the left of the dancers, or seated upon chairs.

2. At the start of the drum beat, 4/4 | ♪♩♪♩ | 160, the three watchers walk to *C* and sit cross-legged upon the ground facing the front.

3. Immediately after the three watchers have seated themselves, the lead dancer, holding the tomahawk in his R hand, dances into the area performing the Toe-Heel step (Chap. 3). He does not move directly to *B* but circles and weaves, taking any course he desires. While dancing he carries his tomahawk in his R hand. He holds it high in the air above his head, and very proudly, he keeps looking at it. Finally, he passes the tomahawk to the left side of his chest and places the head of the tomahawk into his L hand with the shaft hanging down. He repeatedly extends his L arm and then brings his hand back to his chest. He moves the tomahawk across

his chest from left to right and extends his left arm high to the left again. Each time he performs this action he follows the tomahawk with his eyes and his face shows great admiration.

4. From time to time the brave stands still, and holding the tomahawk steady, he proudly glances around. Finally, upon reaching *B*, with his back to the watchers, he stoops and places the tomahawk upon the ground.

5. The lead brave stands erect and dances the Right-Foot Stomp, first to the right and then to the left of the tomahawk. The Right-Foot Stomp is a simple step to perform. The drum beat remains the same.

Right-Foot Stomp

    a. On beat one, the dancer hops low on his L foot and bends his right knee. This action raises his R leg about one foot off the ground.

    b. On beat two the dancer again hops on his L foot and at the same time he stomps his R foot hard upon the ground about one foot in front of the L foot and slightly to the right side of the tomahawk.

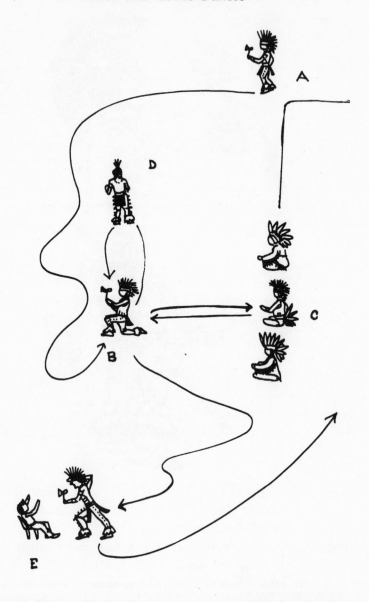

c. On beats three and four the hop and stomp are repeated with the R foot striking the ground to the left of the tomahawk.

6. He repeats procedure 5, again stomping R foot to the right and then to the left side of the tomahawk.

7. After the stomp step, the lead Indian, using four Toe-Heel steps, circles counterclockwise around the tomahawk.

8. He then repeats procedures 5, 6, and 7.

9. Having circled the tomahawk for the second time, the Indian brave, using the Toe-Heel step, dances to the right to *D* where he begins weaving and circling.

10. While the lead dancer circles, the Indian sitting between the other two watchers suddenly crawls forward and picks up the tomahawk and admires it.

11. The lead dancer turns and looks for his tomahawk. Upon seeing the intruder admiring it, the lead dancer charges toward him to regain his property, taking huge steps and making menacing grimaces at the intruder; during this action, the drummer strikes one heavy beat upon the drum when the lead dancer discovers the intruder. The drum is then silent during the rest of the charge.

12. Upon reaching the intruder, the lead dancer utters a loud piercing scream, and placing his hands upon the intruder's shoulders, he pushes him backwards. The intruder drops the tomahawk and crawls back to his position between the other two watchers.

13. The lead Indian picks up his tomahawk, and at the start of the drum beat, using the Toe-Heel step, he dances around the area. While dancing, he keeps admiring his tomahawk and making menacing glances at the intruder.

14. After circling several times around the area, the lead dancer again places his tomahawk upon the ground and repeats the Right-Foot Stomp and the circling actions described in procedures 5, 6, 7, 8, and 9.

15. As the lead dancer again weaves and circles at the right side of the area, the middle watcher sneaks forward on all fours and again steals the tomahawk. He quickly crawls back to his original position between his two friends. Without being seen by the audience, he carefully hides the stolen tomahawk by placing it behind or under one of his friends. His two friends secretly help him to conceal the tomahawk from the dancer and spectators.

16. The lead dancer suddenly turns and glances toward the spot where he had left his tomahawk. Upon seeing that it is gone, he charges again toward the suspected thief, again taking big steps. The drummer strikes one loud beat the instant the lead Indian discovers his tomahawk is missing, and then the drum is silent during the charge. The dancer shoves the middle Indian over, or pulls him away and looks for the stolen tomahawk.

17. Having failed to discover his tomahawk, the lead Indian, using long strides, begins searching for it. During the search the drummer maintains a slow, heavy beat that matches the big steps of the searcher. When searching, the dancer takes four big steps in any desired direction, then stops and, putting one or both hands above his eyes, peers around. This hesitation requires several of the slow drumbeats; the time taken for pause is optional. The searcher repeats the steps and stops several times, finally guiding himself so that he is in front of the audience, at *E*.

18. Unknown to the audience and sitting in the front row is a friend of the lead dancer who has hidden a duplicate tomahawk upon the ground

behind an unsuspecting spectator. The lead performer dances before the audience, and upon recognizing his friend, knows where the duplicate tomahawk is hidden. Suddenly the dancer leaps forward and grasps the hidden tomahawk with his right hand. He raises it high over his head, and uttering a shrill cry, makes a sweep with the tomahawk over the head of the innocent spectator as though scalping him.

19. The basic drum beat is immediately started again and the lead Indian dances from the area. In leaving, he circles and weaves instead of following a straight line. He occasionally glances disdainfully at the innocent spectator. The three watchers arise, and with walking steps, they follow the dancer from the area, taking the original tomahawk with them.

When this dance is performed before a group of unsuspecting people, it is very effective to have the lead dancer's friend seated with them. The element of surprise increases the excitement of the scalping scene.

OLD MAN'S DANCE

(Eastern Woodland)

Theme

Within the culture of the Eastern Woodland Indians was a unique society called the "False Face Society." False faces or masks made of wood or woven grass were worn by their dancers. If the masks were hideous it was to ward off evil spirits, and they were generally worn when the performer was dancing for someone who was ill. For their comedy dances, they wore humorous masks.

Indians, similarly to white men, enjoy comedy and funny situations. The Old Man's Dance is a splendid example of Indian humor. In this dance two braves mimic the slow and shaky movements of old men. All Indians, even the older ones, enjoy the dance and laugh heartily at the two performers as the little one outdoes the taller and stronger man. The disgruntled and impatient acts of the smaller man, plus the funny masks, add greatly to the comedy of the dance.

Outfit

The outfits worn by the dancers may be any standard Indian outfit plus masks which resemble old, tired men. Needed as props are a small wooden branch and a large log. The large log must be hollow and of light weight so that the smaller Indian can easily pick it up and carry it around. The best log for this purpose is one made of papier-mâché.

Procedure

1. The dance is done by two Indians who take the parts of the old men, and two workers. At the start of the slow drum beat, 4/4 | ♪ ♩ ♪ ♩ | 100, the two workers laboriously carry the big log into the area. This slow drum beat is continued throughout the dance. They carefully set the log down and then one of the workers, who helped with the big log and also carried the branch, places the small branch to the left of the log as shown. The workers return to the side of the dance area where they sit down to watch the fun.

2. The two old men are different in size. One is tall and the other is very small and of light structure. After the workers have left the area the tall dancer moves into the area, using a slow Heel-Toe step (Chapter 3); the drum beat remains the same. The dancer is stooped over, his legs are spread wide apart, and his knees are bent and shaky, to represent old

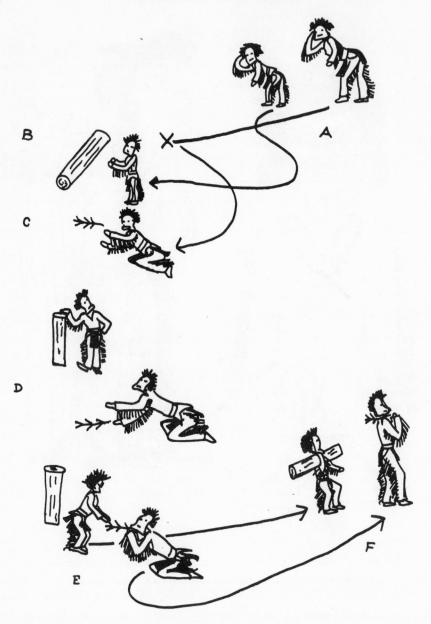

age. His hands are placed above his eyes as he peers around looking for wood. Moving into the area he approaches the log at *B*. Seeing the log, he stops, looks startled, and places his hands out front in a pushing gesture. He shakes his head negatively. He then dances backward 2 steps, turns left, and dances toward the small branch at *C*. He kneels down and tries unsuccessfully to pick up the small branch. During this action the small man, using the Heel-Toe step, dances into the area. He also dances as an old man. He goes to the big log, easily picks it up, and places it upon his left shoulder.

3. The small dancer glances at the tall man who is desperately trying to pick up the little branch. Balancing the log on his shoulder with one hand, the small man dances over to the side of the tall one. He sets the log down on one of its ends and, leaning upon it, taps his foot upon the ground while impatiently watching the taller Indian, who is still having trouble trying to pick up the branch. The tall Indian glances at the little one and makes pleading gestures toward him, and the little Indian turns his head away and ignores his pleas—*D*.

4. The small Indian picks up his log and dances eight steps away from the other Indian. The tall Indian again tries to pick up the branch. Each time he tries, he drops it and falls over backward from the effort.

5. The small Indian again returns to the side of the tall man. He repeats his ignoring of the pleas of the bigger one. The tall man unsuccessfully attempts to pick up the branch, and each time he tries he falls over backward.

6. The dancers repeat three times the above actions of dancing away and returning, pleading and ignoring. The fourth time the small Indian dances away, he stops and places his log upon the ground. He then returns and helps the tall dancer. He places the branch on the shoulder of the tall Indian who staggers, but is finally able to hold it—*E*. The small man retrieves his big log and together they slowly dance from the area—*F*. The workers stand up and walk from the dance area.

RABBIT OR ROUND DANCE

(*Southwest* and *Plains*)

Theme

The Rabbit or Round Dance is typical of many of the social dances of the American Indian. It is simple in structure and is repeated over and over until the dancers tire. Being a simple dance it allows all members of the tribe an opportunity to participate. They usually respond, and it is a common sight to see almost every able person in a tribe dancing at one time. Even the children form their own circles and dance.

As in most Indian social dances, the women are allowed to take part. They participate with enthusiasm and excitement and seem to welcome the opportunity. They lead in the merriment and joviality of the occasion. Their endurance is remarkable and often matches that of the men. Because of the eagerness of Indian men and women to participate in social dances it is surprising that they didn't develop more dances of this type.

Outfits

The dancers wear any of the standard Indian outfits.

Procedure

1. This dance is performed by any number of couples.

2. The couples stand in a straight line without holding hands at *A* or the brave stands in front of his woman partner holding her right hand with his left. His right hand is extended forward, holding the left hand of the woman in front of him. Also it is permissible to use the side position as shown in the illustration of the starting position above.

3. The dancers move from *A* to *B* using a Four-Count Quick-Step, drum beat 4/4 | ♪ ♪ ♪ ♪ | 160.

Four-Count Quick-Step

  a. In the starting position, the feet are held together with the weight of the body upon the right foot. On beat one, the dancer steps his L foot forward about two feet. As the L foot moves forward both arms are moved forward ahead of the body. The dancer bends both knees slightly and leans forward from the hips.

  b. On beat two, which is the heavy beat, the dancer moves his R foot forward about one and a half feet and stomps it hard upon the ground. The arms start to move slightly backward and the body begins to straighten up.

  c. On beat three the dancer steps backward onto his L foot, about twelve inches to the rear, slightly behind the R foot. The arms are still moving backward and the body is slowly resuming an erect position.

  d. On beat four the dancer steps backward onto his R foot, placing it even with the L foot as it was in the starting position. Body is now standing erect and the dancer is in position to repeat the dance step.

The arm and body actions are important in this dance. Remember that both arms swing forward on beat one and the knees are bent and the body is leaning forward. On beats two, three, and four the arms and body are moving backward to their original starting position, except that on beat four both arms of the male dancer are slightly behind his body.

At *B* the lead male dancer with his right hand grasps the left hand of the end female forming a circle. The group continues dancing the quick step and circles indefinitely. The dance continues until the performers are tired. As the dance progresses tired singles or couples may drop out at any time and re-enter when rested.

4. During the dance new couples or singles standing on the outside of the circle may break or cut into the dance. The other dancers are always happy to let them in the line and they laugh and cheer the newcomers.

5. Another part of the dance which causes great merriment is the trapping of an unsuspecting spectator. Anyone in the moving circle may at any opportune time free one of his hands and quickly grasp the hand of a spectator and pull that person into the dance.

6. If the original circle becomes overly large the new dancers often form a concentric circle around the first circle, or form new small circles in the dance area. Sometimes they break up the big circle into several small circles. For variation they often form two circles with the women on the inside and the men on the outside. The circles may both move in the same direction or go opposite to one another.

SQUAW DANCE

(*Navajo*)

Theme

The Navajo Indians did not live in close communities such as their neighbors, the Pueblo people. Their hogans were spread far and wide in their desert setting, and next door neighbors usually lived several miles away. There was a need for the young boys and girls to get together to socialize, and pick mates to carry on the race. They solved this problem by holding a Squaw Dance. The news traveled fast and people came from all over the area to participate.

According to custom a young man had to give the young lady with whom he wished to dance a gift before she would dance with him. Today, the young men usually give money to the lady of their choice.

Outfit

The squaw's outfit is composed of a brightly colored velvet blouse, a long skirt of red, black, turquoise, or purple, a beaded or paint-decorated belt, moccasins, and decorative beads. The male dancer wears white pants split at the bottom Spanish style, belt, brightly colored shirt, moccasins, headband made from a brightly colored neckerchief, necklace, bracelet, and rings.

Procedure

1. The number of couples who may participate in this dance is optional. They line up at *A*, with the girls on the right side of their male partners. The boy places his right arm around the back of his partner and rests his hand on her right shoulder. This is the usual dancing position. However, they sometimes dance while holding inside hands. He holds her left hand with his right. Sometimes they do this dance with the male holding a

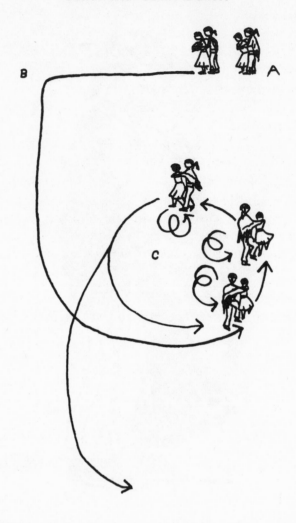

blanket around the shoulders of his partner. He grasps one corner of the blanket with his left hand and places this hand upon his chest. The blanket is placed around his back, and he holds the opposite corner of the blanket in his right hand; he places his right arm around the shoulders of his partner.

2. At the start of the drum beat, the couples dance into the area using a simple forward and backward, or Up-Back, step. At *B* the leading couple turns left and leads the line into a large circle—*C*. The drum beat throughout this dance is slow and steady, 4/4 | ♩ ♩ ♩ ♩ | 120.

Up-Back Step

   a. On beat one, each dancer steps forward with the L foot about twelve inches ahead of the R foot.

   b. On beat two, they step forward with the R foot and place it down with the R toe even with the heel of the L foot.

c. On beat three, the L foot is stepped backward and placed down so that the toe of the L foot is slightly ahead of the R heel.

d. On beat four, the R foot is raised about five inches from the ground and immediately lowered to receive the weight. Do not step back or forward on this fourth step.

The distance one steps with the L foot on beat one determines the forward progress of the dancer.

3. At the completion of the circle, the drum beat stops and the couples stand in place. The drummer resumes the beat, and the dancers do three Up-Back steps and move forward around the circle.

4. After the three Up-Back steps, the dancers perform in place an Up-Side-and-Back step. This requires six drum beats. The drummer does not change his rhythm but continues the steady beat as used for the simple Up-Back step, and the dancers adapt the six beat step to the continuous rhythm.

Up-Side-and-Back Step—Six-Beat

a. On beat one, each dancer steps forward with the L foot about two feet—Fig. 1.

b. On beat two, the dancer raises his R foot about three inches above the ground and then replaces it—Fig. II.

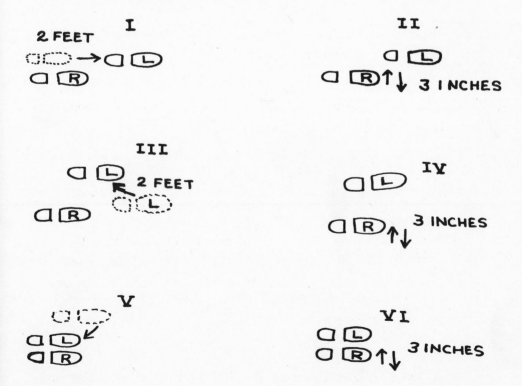

c. On beat three, the dancer steps sideward about two feet and backward about one foot with his L foot—Fig. III.

d. On beat four, the dancer repeats the raising and lowering of his R foot as in 4*b*—Fig. IV.

e. On beat five, the dancer steps diagonally backward with the L foot, placing it beside the R foot—Fig. V.

f. On beat six, the dancer repeats the raising and lowering actions of the R foot—Fig. VI.

5. Dancers repeat the six beat, Up-Side-and-Back step as performed in procedure 4.

6. Couples repeat three Up-Back steps moving forward around the circle.

7. The dancers continue the Up-Back step six more times while pivoting counterclockwise. The male moves the girl around with him as he dances the pivot. She takes big steps to keep up with her partner.

Repeat the above procedures 4, 5, 6, and 7 as many times as desired. The length of this dance is optional. Couples can drop out, enter or re-enter as desired.

7

War and Skill Dances

BOW AND ARROW DANCE
(Southwest)

Theme

The bow and arrow was a weapon that contributed vitally to the Indians' way of life; it was used long before and even after the white man came to America; it was used as a hunting weapon and as an implement of war. The Indians gained great skill in the use of the weapon. The Bow and Arrow Dance was performed to demonstrate this skill and also to pay tribute to the weapon which was so important to their existence.

Outfit

The Bow and Arrow dancer usually wears a feather roach, war skirt, pants or leggings, and moccasins, and carries a bow and arrow. However, it is permissible to wear any standard Indian outfit and carry a bow and arrow.

Procedure

1. This dance is performed by five to ten braves who stand in a single line at *A;* they hold bow at shoulder or chest height with the arrow in shooting position. For protection the bow is held loosely and not drawn.

2. At the start of the drum beat, the braves dance to *B*, using the One-Foot Stomp (Chap. 3) drum beat 4/4 | ♪ ♩ ♪ ♩ | 140–180, depending upon the ability of the dancers.

3. At *B*, the dancers continue the One-Foot Stomp in place. They execute a tracking movement.

Tracking

   a. The first four stomp steps are done while the Indians stand erect, facing the original line of direction.

   b. During the next two steps, the Indians bend forward, and lowering the bow, they touch the point of the arrow upon the ground; during the next two steps, they rise to the erect position.

   c. During the next four steps, the dancers make a quarter turn left.

d. They then repeat *b*, bending, touching the arrow point, and standing erect.

e. During the next four steps the Indians make a quarter turn right, and using four more steps, they repeat the touching of the arrow to the ground.

f. During the next four steps the dancers make a quarter turn right, and using four steps, they again repeat the touching of the arrow to the ground.

g. During the next four steps they turn left, resuming their original directions.

4. Using the One-Foot Stomp, the line moves forward four steps, and then the first Indian in the line turns or circles left. The other Indians

follow him until they are at *C*, in a straight line, but facing opposite to the directions they were at *B*.

5. They then repeat procedure 3, the dancing in place and the tracking movements.

6. Then they repeat procedure 4, but circling the dancers to right—*D*.

7. At *D*, they repeat procedure 3.

8. Continuing the One-Foot Stomp, the line turns left, and the Indians dance from the area.

FEATHER DANCE

(*Plains*)

Theme

In sports and other activities, competition is used as a tool or method for increasing interest and motivating participants to practice and improve their skills and abilities. Non-Indian cultures have used competition, not only to improve interest and skill, but also, by keeping scores, to determine winners. This practice was never popular among the Indians. Seldom did they keep a score; they pitted themselves against each other or against something in nature, to defeat or overcome an obstacle, but not to determine a champion as we do today.

The Feather Dance was a skill dance in which each dancer attempted to overcome an obstacle in nature. It was developed to give the warrior a chance to improve and display his skills of speed, coordination, and balance. The warriors spent many hours of practice to develop the skill required in the Feather Dance. They perfected their skill until they somewhat resembled a fast-flying bird that suddenly hesitates in its flight and swoops down to the earth to snatch with its beak an unsuspecting prey, and then flies proudly away with it.

Outfit

The outfit is composed of a feather or hair roach or a war bonnet, arm bands, arm cuffs, breechclout, leg and ankle bells, fetlocks, and moccasins, or any standard war dance outfit. The large back bustle can be worn to add color and variation to the outfit. A feather is placed standing upright in the center of the dance area at *C*.

Procedure

1. This dance is done by several male dancers, who line up in a straight

line, one behind the other, at *A*.

2. At the start of the drum beat, the dancers, using a fast Foot-and-Heel Shuffle (Chap. 3) drum beat 8/8 | ♩ ♩ ♪ ♪ ♪♪ | 180, proceed to *B*. Simultaneously, they dance a quarter turn left, so that they are facing the feather standing upright at *C*.

3. The first Indian dances toward the feather using a Toe-Toe-Heel or a Toe-Heel step (Chap. 3) drum beat 4/4 | ♩ ♩ ♩ ♩ | 140.

The Toe-Toe-Heel step is a variation of the Toe-Heel. The dancer taps his toe two times, very fast, instead of once. He taps the toe twice to one drum beat.

He does not go directly to the feather, but circles and weaves while progressing toward it. Suddenly, he doubles the time of his footsteps and charges straight to the feather. The drummer does not change or speed up his beat, but the dancer increases his tempo. Upon reaching the feather he quickly bends low and makes an attempt to grasp the feather between his teeth and then dance away with it. During his attempt to snatch the feather he can hesitate slightly, but the Indian who hesitates little or none at all is more vigorously cheered by the other dancers and spectators. During the snatching of the feather, the Indian cannot allow any part of his body to touch the ground except his feet.

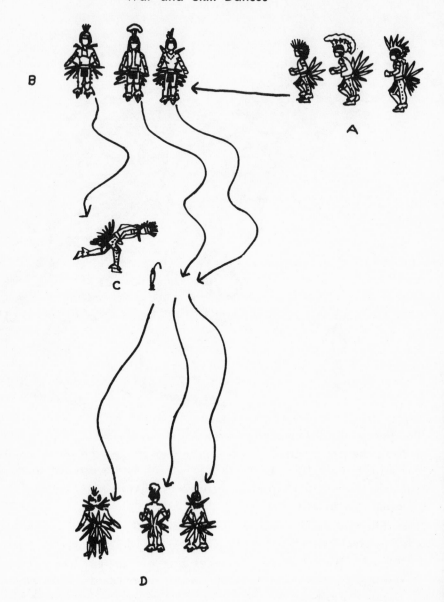

4. After a dancer has successfully picked up the feather with his teeth he takes it in his hand and proudly puts it back in place. He then dances to D where he remains while the other dancers attempt to accomplish the feat. If a dancer fails to obtain the feather, he returns to his place in line and waits for his next turn. The drum beat is continuous throughout the dance and does not stop between different dancers.

5. As each dancer moves forward to make his attempt at the feather, he is applauded and spurred on by the spectators and other dancers with cries, yells, and coyote yaps and yelps. The spectators cry out and cheer loudly when one of the dancers secures the feather.

6. The dance continues until all the dancers have obtained the feather and have gathered at *D*. They then dance from the area using the Toe-Toe-Heel step.

HOOP DANCE—SIMPLE, OR SINGLE-HOOP

(*Most Tribes*)

Theme

Some of the first Indian tribes to dance the Hoop Dance were the Chippewa. They lived around Lake Minnesota, and from the young pliable branches of willows, which grew abundantly in the area, they fashioned their hoops. When first performed by these people the hoop was manipulated over the body without the use of the hands. The dance grew out of the concept that man and his desires are never satisfied; that he continually seeks to develop increased skill and improved and different ways of doing things.

The American Indians love to dance, so it was natural that they ventured into new ideas and ways of dancing. From the shores of Lake Minnesota the Hoop Dance spread south and southwest throughout America. Today it is one of the most popular dances performed by the Indian tribes in those areas.

The Hoop Dance is an exhibition of how skillfully one can maneuver his body through and around a hoop while keeping his dance step steady and in time with the rhythm of the drum. Because of the skill required to perform this dance the Indians often refer to it as their "Spectacular."

Outfit

The dancer wears a stripped down war dance outfit. The outfit should be simple, in order not to interfere with the movement of the hoop. He usually wears a hair roach, breechclout, arm bands, fetlocks, ankle bells, and moccasins. The hoop is of light material and about one inch in circumference. The diameter of the hoop varies with the size of the dancer; the average hoop being about 30 inches.

Procedure

1. The hoop is placed upon the ground in the center of the dance area. The hoop is not perfectly level, but is slightly bent on one side. When placed down the bent edge is toward the dancer. The bent edge, facing the dancer, should curve up off the ground about two inches. When this raised

edge is stepped on by the dancer the opposite side of the hoop leaves the ground. Dancers who do not use the uneven hoop, step upon one edge of it and brush the foot backward, thus rolling the round edge of the hoop toward them and lifting the other edge from the floor.

2. At the start of the drum beat, which remains the same throughout the dance, the performer, using the Toe-Heel step (Chap. 3) drum beat 4/4 | ♩ ♩ ♩ ♩ | 160, moves into the dance area. He dances directly over to the hoop at *B*, and places the toe of his R foot upon the raised edge of the hoop. This action raises the opposite edge, under which he quickly slides his L foot. Bending low he grasps the hoop with his L hand and draws it up and around his L leg until it is at crotch height. The L hand holds the hoop forward and away from the front of the body.

3. The dancer now places his head, R arm, and shoulders through the hoop—C. He straightens his body as the hoop slides over his shoulders and both arms and down his body. At waist height, the dancer grasps the hoop

with his R hand and releases his L hand hold. The hoop is now at crotch height and around the R leg. It is in an exact opposite position from that at the end of procedure 2.

4. Procedure 3 is repeated with opposite leg, arm, and body movements, the hoop returning to the L leg.

5. With the hoop around the L leg and held with the L hand, the dancer grasps the hoop on the opposite side with the R hand. With both hands holding the hoop, the dancer raises his R leg and steps into the hoop—D. The hoop is lowered until the rear edge is touching the back of the knees. The head is ducked forward and down through the hoop—E. The body is straightened so that the hoop will slide off, by way of the back of the body— F.

6. The L hand releases the hoop and the R hand grasps it, holding it

low in front of the body. The dancer steps into the hoop, first with his R foot and then with his L foot and pulls the hoop up to waist height, holding it with both hands; he lowers the edge of the hoop, which is at the rear of the body, to knee height and again puts his head and shoulders forward through the hoop; he stands up and releases the hoop from the body, repeating procedure 5—*D, E,* and *F.*

7. Procedure 6 is repeated. (Three times the dancer stoops forward through the hoop).

8. Standing erect and holding the hoop in the R hand, the dancer swings the hoop down past the right side of his body and then to the rear; he brings the hoop quickly forward to the front and releases it, allowing it to roll forward, but putting a reverse spinning action on the roll. The hoop will proceed several feet in front of the performer, who is dancing toward it. Suddenly it will reverse its direction and roll back toward the dancer; and upon reaching the spinning hoop, the performer places his R foot through the R side of the hoop and grasps it with his R hand—*G.* He immediately raises the hoop up his R leg to crotch height. The action of placing head, shoulders, arms and body through hoop, as described in procedure 3, is repeated—*H.*

9. Upon straightening the body, the dancer releases both hands from the hoop. This allows the hoop to slide down the L leg and rest upon the ground.

10. The dancer removes his L foot from the hoop. Stooping low, he picks up the hoop with his R hand and takes the hoop around the right side of his body until it is directly behind him with the bottom or lower edge of the hoop approximately even with the back of the knees. In this position, the dancer grasps the hoop with his L hand; it is now held with both hands. The dancer stoops forward and at the same time sits backward through the hoop. The top of the hoop is allowed to fall forward as it comes over his head—*I.* The hoop is now around his body at about knee height. Releasing the hoop, the dancer allows it to fall to the ground. He steps from the hoop, first with the L foot, then with the R foot.

11. Procedure 10 is repeated.

12. The dancer removes his feet from the fallen hoop and dances around the area; he again approaches the hoop and the entire dance is repeated three more times, at the end of which he keeps the hoop in his R hand and dances from the area—*J.* As the dancers gain skill in performing this dance, the tempo can be increased from 160 to 200 counts per minute.

RATTLE DANCE

(*Plains*)

Theme

Indian dancers enjoy shaking rattles as they dance; they shake their rattles in time with the drum beats and with their own rhythmical body movements. The rattles are not only used to accent and emphasize the rhythmic beat but to add tonal color and beauty to the dance. A good rattle must have a pleasing tone and be decorated with bright colors and feathers. Indians usually make their rattles from gourds, leather, wood, horns, and shells.

The Rattle Dance is ordinarily performed by an Indian brave who has just completed making a beautiful set of rattles which he desires to show, in all their beauty, to the other tribesmen. While he dances, the Indian proudly displays his rattles while performing graceful head, arm, leg, and body movements; he takes great pride in his dancing skill and in his ability to shake the rattles in time with the drum beats and with his foot and body actions.

Outfit

The rattle dancer may wear any standard war dance outfit and carry two hand rattles. The war dance outfit shown is composed of a feather roach, arm and wrist cuffs, breechclout, back bustle, knee, leg or ankle bells, fetlocks, rattles, and moccasins, and the dancer has painted designs on the body.

Procedure

1. The dancer moves from *A* to *B*, using a forward, Toe-Heel step (Chap. 3) drum beat 4/4 | ♪ ♪ ♪ ♪ | 160. While dancing, the performer continuously shakes the rattles in time with the drum beat; as he shakes he alternately moves his arms in a circle. Starting with both arms held in front of the body, the right arm is raised upward, then backward and downward, and then upward to its original position. The windmill action of the arm is to the side of the body. While the arm is circling, the rattle is shaken and the dancer turns his head and keeps his eyes on the rattle. At the time the right arm reaches the front position, the left arm begins its circling action. The brave now turns his head and follows the left arm with his eyes. Remember that both rattles are being continuously shaken.

2. At *B* the dancer continues his Toe-Heel step but changes the pattern of his arm actions; he first raises his right hand upward above eye level, and raising his head, he proudly admires the rattle. He then slowly lowers it to

the front position. He now repeats this action with his left hand. Remember that both rattles are shaken continuously during this action. This action requires twelve Toe-Heel steps and moves the dancer from *B* to *C*.

3. At *C* the brave dances in place, and leaning forward, he places his rattles upon the ground in front of him. Straightening his body, he begins hopping upon his L foot; he extends his R foot forward, and in time with the hop, he taps his R toe first to the right of the rattles, then to their left. He then repeats this action to the right and left of the rattles. The dancer repeats the above action on the opposite foot, hopping four times upon his R foot while tapping his L foot once to the left of the rattles, to their right, and to their left and to their right again.

4. Beginning again the Toe-Heel step in place, the brave bends forward and picks up his rattles; he shakes them as he slowly resumes his upright position (the time required is optional).

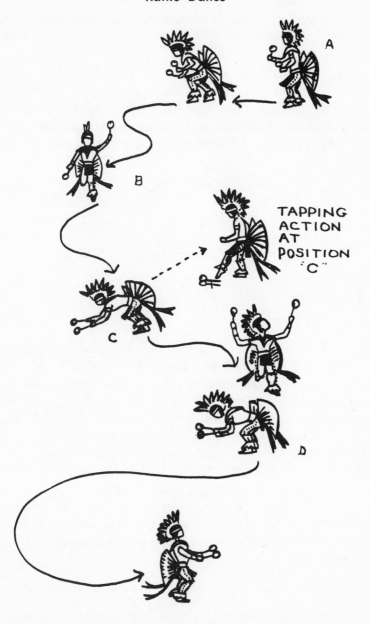

TAPPING
ACTION
AT
POSITION
"C"

5. The brave dances to *D* (optional point), continuously shaking his rattles and repeating side arm circling as in procedure 1.

6. At *D* the brave stops dancing, and with hands held together, he slowly bends forward and touches the rattles to the ground; then he slowly raises the rattles from the floor and resumes his standing position; he shakes the rattles while lowering and raising them. Remember that the shaking of the rattles is always in time with the drum beat. The time required to lower and raise the rattles is optional and depends upon the dancer; most dancers require about 32 drum beats to complete this movement.

7. In a standing position, the dancer makes a complete counterclockwise circle with the right arm and then with the left arm, keeping the rattles shaking.

8. Procedures 6 and 7 are repeated.

9. The brave dances from the area, shaking his rattles which are held in front of the body at about hip level. Throughout the dance the drum beat is continuous and the rhythm, tempo, and accent remain the same. If the 160 tempo is too fast for beginner dancers, it may be slowed to 120 to 140 counts per minute.

SCALP DANCE

(*Sioux*)

Theme

The Sioux Indians were some of the finest horsemen and fighters of the plains Indians. The Sioux were well known for their taking of scalps. The taking of scalps was never meant to be a form of torture or inhumanity, but represented a trophy or souvenir of battle. Generally, only a lock of the scalp was taken and not the entire hair as sometimes believed. Just as the white man marked his airplane during the war to recount his conquests, so did the Indian mark his teepee with scalps to display his deeds and ability in battle.

The dance shows a young Sioux warrior as he tracks and stalks the enemy; it depicts him moving along quietly, listening to the ground for noises, and checking the wind for direction. The climax of the dance is brought about by his overwhelming the enemy (or coup) and the taking of the scalp trophy.

Outfit

The Scalp Dance performer may wear any standard war dance outfit, and carry a tomahawk and have a scalp lock or braid of hair hidden under his belt. A feather roach, and leg or ankle bells, add to this dance.

Procedure

1. The brave dances from *A* to *B*, using the War Dance step, the Variation step, or the Cross-Over Sti-yu (Chap. 3) drum beat 4/4 | ♩ ♩ ♩ ♩ | 120. He holds his tomahawk in his left hand and carries it about waist high. Occasionally, he points the tomahawk to the earth as though tracking and following footsteps.

2. At *B*, the dancer stops and kneels down. He lowers his head and places his ear to the ground and listens for the sound of footsteps. The drummer continues the beat, but very softly.

3. The brave resumes the kneeling position and, with his right hand, checks the direction of the wind. He picks up dirt and allows it to sift through his fingers as he studies its movements.

4. The brave repeats procedures 1, 2, and 3 three more times; during the repetitions he continuously holds the tomahawk pointed toward the footprints upon the ground in front of him.

5. During the last repeat, the dancer guides himself so that upon kneeling, he is directly in front of the audience. He lowers his head to listen, and while doing this, without revealing his actions to the audience he removes with his right hand the hidden scalp from his belt.

6. The drummer strikes a loud beat upon the drum and the dancer

leaps forward with his tomahawk held high over his head—C. He grasps the hair of an unsuspecting person in the audience, and uttering a piercing scream, makes a sweeping motion with the tomahawk as though scalping the person.

7. The brave raises the false scalp over his head, and using a fast Toe-Heel step (Chap. 3) drum beat 4/4 | ♪ ♪ ♪ ♪ | 160, circles three times before the audience. While circling, he utters several war whoops ("Eeeeee-yah") and shakes the scalp at the audience.

8. The brave runs or dances from the area, during which time he shakes the scalp over his own head; two or three times during the exit he hesitates, and looking back over his shoulder, he utters the war cry while furiously shaking the scalp. If it is not practical to have the brave scalp an unsuspecting spectator, the scalp can be placed upon a three foot post standing upright in the dance area. The brave charges the pole and removes the scalp from it, and the dance remains otherwise the same.

SHAKE DANCE

(Shoshone)

Theme

The Shoshone dancing place was not a large dance hall, as in the white man's society, but nature herself. His roof was the great sky and his floor the earth. When a group of dancers performed the war dance, much dust was stirred up and each dancer became very dusty, and so he often stopped to shake off the dust. As time went on the Shoshones, as well as other Indian Tribes, used this idea to develop the Shake Dance.

In this dance, there is usually more than one dancer. The participants, upon entering the area, form a circle, and it is exciting fun to watch them performing the fast rhythmic war dance steps. Many times during the dance the drumming is abruptly stopped and the Indians, maintaining their last body and foot positions, begin to shake and quiver. It is not only fun to watch them shake and to imagine the dust being shaken off, but it is very pleasing to the ears to hear the rhythmic and beautiful tones of the leg and ankle bells worn by the dancers.

Outfit

In this dance any simple Indian outfit may be worn. Refer to the outfit worn for the Kiowa War Dance at the end of this chapter or the Sioux
Scalp Dance just above. No matter how simple the outfit, leg and ankle
bells are required.

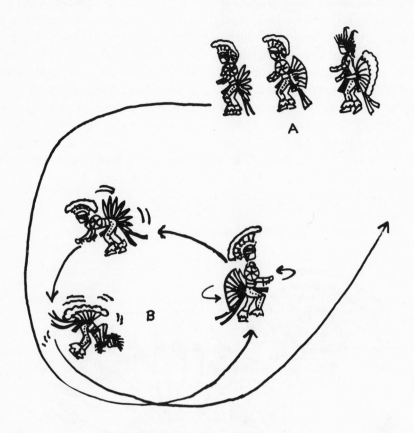

Procedure

1. At *A*, the dancers line up, one behind the other. The number of
dancers is optional but usually involves about 20 men.

2. At the start of the drum beat, the dancers either walk or dance using
the Heel-Toe step, Toe-Heel step, or Heel Shuffle (Chap. 3) drum beat 4/4
| ♪ ♩ ♪ ♩ | 160, to *B* and form a circle. If many dancers are used, several
small circles are formed rather than one large. After the circle is formed,
the men stop dancing and turn in place, facing outward. During the rest
of the dance, the performers maintain the circle and remain in their relative
positions. They do not mix nor do they proceed around the circle.

3. When the drumming resumes (with the same beat) the dancers, using
the Heel-Toe step, circle in place counterclockwise or clockwise. The
dancers perform separately and change the direction of their circling as

desired; also, according to their own wishes, they weave and turn from side to side and crouch or stand erect.

4. When the drumming stops, each dancer remains in his last position, places his hands upon his hips with the thumbs to the rear, bends over and shakes or quivers his entire body. As he shakes the dust from his body, his leg and ankle bells ring out clearly.

5. When the drumming resumes again, the dancers continue the Heel-Toe step and the turning in place as in procedure 3. The timing of the drum stops and starts is optional and is left up to the discretion of the drummer. After the dancers have repeated the circling and shaking about five times (optional), the lead dancer turns from the circle, and followed by the other dancers, he leads them from the dance area.

SPEAR AND SHIELD DANCE

(Plains)

Theme

The Indians made strong shields from the shoulder hide of the buffalo. Four to five layers of the tough hide were stretched over a wooden frame, making it so durable and heavy that a flying arrow, thrown tomahawk, or spear could not penetrate it. Great skill was acquired by the Indians in the use of the shields to protect themselves. They often danced to show their skill and ability in the use of the shield and to demonstrate their cunning with war implements.

Two warriors attired in full war dress and carrying a spear and shield participate in the Spear and Shield Dance. They face one another and go through the motions of two warriors fighting. The warlike actions of charging, thrusting the spears, and warding them off with the shields are skillfully executed by the two braves. Following the combative actions, the fighters proudly wave their spears, while performing a fast war dance. The war dance signifies that skill has brought about victory.

Outfit

The dancer's outfit includes a Mandan horned bonnet, or a war bonnet, with a long feathered trailer, a spear and a shield. The rest of his outfit can be any standard war dance dress. The shield can be made from cardboard, thin masonite or plywood decorated with designs and feathers. Attach two straps or tie-strings to the back of the shield for holding. The spear can be made from an old broom handle or stick. Sew or tack over the

face of the shield a heavy cloth cover and sew feathers to the cloth. Do not sharpen the spear but leave it blunt for safety.

Procedure

1. The braves dance from *A* to *B*, using a Foot-and-Heel Shuffle (Chap. 3) drum beat 8/8 | ♩ ♩ ♪ ♪ ♪ ♪ ♪ | 120. At *B*, they stop dancing and stand side by side. For the correct positions of the shield and spear, see the diagram.

2. When the beating of the drum resumes, 10/8 | ♪ ♪ ♪ ♪ ♪ ♪ ♪ ♪. | 200, the dancers run forward seven quick steps to *C* and stop. They immediately thrust their spears, point forward, toward the front and slightly

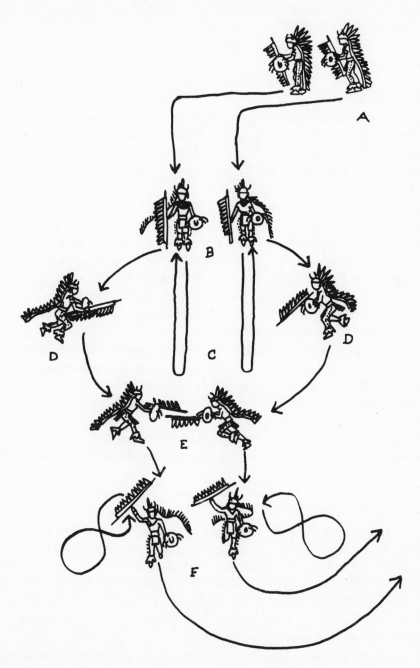

sideward and away from each other. The running step is performed on the balls of the feet and the steps are short and quick. The thrust is made on the eighth beat, which is three times longer than any of the quick drum beats.

3. After the thrust, the spear is returned to the side of the dancer, with its head pointing upward. The dancers pivot away from each other and,

using seven fast running steps, return to *B*. On the eighth drum beat they again repeat the spear thrust.

4. At *B*, and still facing in the direction of the second run, the dancers bend forward from the hips and move their shields and spears back and forth in front of their bodies; while doing this movement, they eye one another suspiciously.

5. The dancers slowly raise their spears over their right shoulders to a throwing position; then holding the spears in this position, they start performing a Toe-Heel step (Chap. 3) drum beat 4/4 | ♪ ♩ ♪ ♩ | 120; dancing away from each other, but always keeping alert, watching the opponent, the braves dance and circle from *B* to *D*.

6. At *D*, which is an optional distance from *B*, the dancers execute a charge movement. Upon reaching each other at *E*, the dancers stop their forward movement, and immediately thrust their spears at each other's shield; the thrust must strike the shield so that the spear glances from it, with no attempt to strike the body of the opponent. During the charge, the dancers utter a shrill war whoop ("Eeeeeyaaah"). The drum beat during this action remains the same as it was in procedure 5, but the dancers do two steps to each beat of the drum.

7. The dancers turn away from each other and, using the Toe-Heel step, return to *D*; they do not return directly to *D*, but circle and weave in that general direction. At all times the braves keep an eye on one another, because either dancer may charge his opponent at any time. It isn't necessary to make the charge from the original *D;* the dancers usually separate to a distance from which several charge steps are required before contact. No matter which brave charges first, the other must be ready to accept his charge and move immediately toward him.

8. Procedure 7 is repeated two more times. The drum beat never ceases or changes during procedures 6, 7, and 8.

9. At the end of the fourth charge, the braves dance a few feet away from one another to *E* and, facing front, dance in place, using the Toe-Heel step. During the steps, they place their shields upon their chests, and holding the spears outward and sideward, they move their arms and spears in a figure-eight movement. As they start the second figure-eight movement, they lower the shields to their sides. The spears are moved through the figure-eight movement four complete times.

10. Finishing the figure-eight movements, the braves raise their R arms sideward and upward until their spears are directly above their heads, with the points facing forward. Holding the spears in this position, the braves pivot counterclockwise four complete times. In making each pivot, the dancers hop eight times upon the L foot and turn as they hop. At each hop,

the toe of the R foot is tapped upon the ground about one foot ahead of the L foot and slightly to the side.

11. After the dancers complete the four pivots, the steady drum beat is terminated and the dancers lower their spears and walk side by side from the dance area.

WAR DANCE

(*Kiowa*)

Theme

The white man has his pep rallies to whip up enthusiasm and to spur his team to victory. Similarly, the Indians had their war dances to prepare their braves for the fight and to pray for victory in the battle. They not only danced to build enthusiasm, but used the dance as an opportunity to display their knowledge of different dance steps, their cunning and skill in the use of their war implements and their physical prowess and endurance. When performing the war dances, the braves wore their most beautiful and colorful outfits.

Today's Indian war dances are not performed to build enthusiasm for war, but are participated in for fun, amusement, and cultural significance. The braves still dance in their most beautiful outfits and enjoy displaying their skill, strength, and endurance and their knowledge of the various complicated war dance steps; they perform their war dances to a very fast tempo with many braves taking part. It is interesting and exciting to watch the many dancers and the various steps and body movements going on all at the same time.

In contrast to the above mentioned war dances, some are very formal in their structure. The dancers follow a definite pattern and use similar steps. One of the most beautiful and representative of the informal type is the Kiowa War Dance. In this dance, a simple and easy method of starting it is employed, and each dancer is given complete freedom of movement and selection of dance steps. The Kiowa braves use the simple basic dance steps, but for variation add many crossovers and turns; and they seldom travel in a straight line. The dancers weave in and out, circle, and move smoothly without interfering with one another. The performers display ability and endurance, and often dance for many minutes without repeating a step. When watching this dance, the spectators are thrilled with the lovely outfits, the precision of the steps, and often wish they could do the impossible and watch each dancing picture of color, rhythm, and originality.

Outfit

The outfit for this dance may be any simple Indian outfit with breechclout, ankle bells, headband, rattle, and moccasins. The outfit shown is
fairly authentic, and magnificent. The parts of this outfit are a feathered
roach, full sized arm and back bustles, feathered wand, cuffs, fetlocks, leg
bells, and knee fur pieces.

Procedure

1. The Kiowa War Dance is performed by many individual participants
(number optional) who walk into the dance area and slowly move around.
They do not bunch up or gather in groups or make any definite formation.

2. At the start of the drum beat 4/4 | ♪ ♩ ♪ ♩ | 180, each participant begins dancing, using steps of his own choice. They adapt the steps of their choice to the basic, fast drum beat. If the 180 tempo is too fast, it may be cut to as slow as 140. It is fascinating to watch many different dancers each employing a different step, yet all in time with the basic beat. The usual basic dance steps used (refer to Chap. 3) are: Heel-Toe, Toe-Heel, Heel Shuffle, Four-Beat Stomp, War Dance, Canoe, and the Cross-Over Sti-yu, and variations and combinations of these steps. The dance continues until participants tire and quit.

3. The braves dance separate patterns and do not interfere with one another. The general direction of the movement of the group, regardless of their individual circling, weaving, sideward, backward, and forward movements, is usually counterclockwise around the dance area.

The following variations of the Toe-Heel dance step are good examples of how the Indians adapt the basic steps to their own liking. Ordinarily the Toe-Heel step is performed using alternate foot action, usually progressing along a straight forward line. In the Kiowa War Dance the performers often double the action of the step and do a Toe-Toe-Heel-Heel pattern instead of the simple Toe-Heel. They might also keep one foot forward, and while doing the step, pivot on the rear foot, and move in a small circle, thus eliminating the alternate foot action. The dancer might vary this step by going sideward, backward, or forward, instead of circling.

Another beautiful variation of this step is the Cross-Over. In this step, the dancer performs the Toe-Toe-Heel-Heel action while alternately crossing the forward foot over the other foot. For example, while hopping on the left foot, the dancer places his right foot forward and over to the left side of the left foot as he does the step. Sometimes the more expert dancers use the Cross-Over step while circling. With diligent practice, concentration, and the use of one's own natural ability, many variations of the basic steps described in Chapter 3 can be developed by young and inexperienced dancers. It is suggested that young dancers be given great freedom in developing their own variations of the basic war dance steps.